ZINN

FOR · BEGINNERS®

ZINN
FOR BEGINNERS®

by **DAVID COGSWELL**
illustrations by **JOE LEE**

FOR BEGINNERS®

an imprint of Steerforth Press
Hanover, New Hampshire

For Beginners LLC
62 East Starrs Plain Road
Danbury, CT 06810 USA
www.forbeginnersbooks.com

A For Beginners® Documentary Comic Book
Copyright © 2009

Cataloging-in-Publication information is available from the Library of Congress.

ISBN # 978-1-934389-40-9 Trade

Manufactured in the United States of America

For Beginners® and Beginners Documentary Comic Books® are published
by For Beginners LLC.

First Edition

10 9 8 7 6 5 4 3 2 1

Table of Contents

Introduction: Zinn's World

Rebel with a Cause

I start from the supposition that the world is topsy-turvy, that things are all wrong, that the wrong people are in jail and the wrong people are out of jail, that the wrong people are in power and the wrong people are out of power, that the wealth is distributed in this country and the world in such a way as not simply to require small reform but to require a drastic re-allocation of wealth.

I start from the supposition that we don't have to say too much about this because all we have to do is think about the state of the world today and realize that things are all upside down. Daniel Berrigan is in jail—A Catholic priest, a poet who opposes the war—and J. Edgar Hoover is free, you see. David Dellinger, who has opposed war ever since he was this high and who has used all of his energy and passion against it, is in danger of going to jail. The men who are responsible for the My Lai massacre are not on trial; they are in Washington serving various functions, primary and subordinate, that have to do with the unleashing of massacres, which surprise them when they occur. At Kent State University four students were killed by the National Guard and students were indicted. In every city in this country, when demonstrations take place, the protesters, whether they have demonstrated or not, whatever they have done, are assaulted and clubbed by police, and then they are arrested for assaulting a police officer.

—Howard Zinn,
"The Problem is Civil Obedience," 1970

Ten years after writing the above words, Howard Zinn published *A People's History of the United States*, which asserts that the history traditionally told in history books is the story told from the standpoint of rulers to justify why they—a tiny percent of humanity—control almost all of the resources. Winston Churchill said, "History is written by the victors." Zinn set out to tell the story from the point of view of the other people in the world, the majority of people, the working, struggling masses. His book set off a revolution—a paradigm shift—in the study of American history.

Zinn does not set out to be objective or impartial and does not claim to be. He begins with a definite point of view and a set of beliefs to which he is dedicated, essentially the same principles that were proclaimed during the Enlightenment and in accordance with the "unalienable rights" to "life, liberty and the pursuit of happiness" articulated in the American Declaration of Independence. Though beautifully stated in the founding documents of America, they are principles that are often scuttled to the margins in the conduct of government and society.

Zinn recognized that any history is selective. The events of the world in any given day could fill many books. Every historian must choose his province that he wishes to explore. Many histories focus on wars and political struggles, some on culture and art. Zinn focuses on the lives and struggles of working people in a developing capitalist society, concentrating on the majority of the population instead of on the thin upper crust of the elites who enjoy the attention of most common historical accounts.

"There was never, for me as a teacher and writer, an obsession with 'objectivity,' which I considered neither possible nor desirable," wrote Zinn in the introduction to *The Zinn Reader*. "I understood early that what is presented as 'history' or as 'news' is inevitably a selection out of an infinite amount of information, and that what is selected depends on what the selector thinks is important."

Marx and Zinn

Some detractors have called Zinn a Marxist. "A guide to the political left" posted at Discover the Networks (www.discoverthenetworks.com), calls *A People's History of the United States* "a Marxist tract which describes America as a predatory and repressive capitalist state—sexist, racist, imperialist—that is run by a corporate ruling class for the benefit of the rich." The site finds it appalling that the book is "one of the best-selling history books of all time. Despite its lack of footnotes and other scholarly apparatus, it is one of most influential texts in college classrooms

3

today—not only in history classes, but also in such fields as economics, political science, literature, and women's studies."

Daniel J. Flynn, the executive director of Accuracy in Academia and author of *Why the Left Hates America: Exposing the Lies That Have Obscured Our Nation's Greatness,* wrote on the History News Network (http://hnn.us/articles/1493.html) that Zinn is an "unreconstructed, anti-American Marxist." Flynn included Zinn on a list of five thousand "Marxists" he said were teaching in American universities.

Upon learning he was included on this list, Zinn rejected Flynn's claim, noting that even Marx himself claimed to not be a Marxist.

In Zinn's article "Je ne suis pas Marxiste," he writes that Marx was invited to speak at the Karl Marx Club in London, but he declined, saying, "Thanks for inviting me to speak at your Karl Marx Club, but I can't. I'm not a Marxist."

Zinn called the incident "a high point" in Marx's life and a good starting point from which to consider Marx's ideas without becoming a Pieper [the founder of the Karl Marx Club] or a Stalin or a Kim Il Sung or any born-again Marxist who argues that every word in Volumes One, Two, and Three, and especially *Grundrisse,* is unquestionably true."

Zinn continued, "For a long time I considered that there were important and useful ideas in Marxist philosophy and political economy." But Marx was also "often wrong, often dogmatic." He was "sometimes too accepting of imperial domination as 'progressive,' a way of bringing capitalism faster to the third world, and therefore hastening, he thought, the road to socialism." On the other hand, Marx "had something to say not only as a critic of capitalism but as a warning to revolutionaries, who had better revolutionize themselves if they intended to do that to society."

Though Zinn does not consider himself a devotee of Marxist ideology, he clearly owes a debt to Marx in terms of his view of history and his analysis of the forces involved in human progress. Marx began his book, *The Communist Manifesto,* by saying: "The history of all hitherto existing society is the history of class struggles." Marx analyzed history in terms of the evolution of societies, an idea adapted from Hegel that was relatively new in Marx's time. And Marx viewed that progression through the lens of economics and economically defined classes.

Practically every modern historian or political scientist owes a debt to Marx. Zinn particularly makes use of Marx's lens on history. So while he is not a Marxist, it is fair to say that Zinn's view is Marxian, to some extent.

Flynn attributed the "massive sales figures" of *A People's History of the United States* to plugs from "fawning celebrities," such as Pearl Jam's Eddie Vedder, the band Rage Against the Machine, and actor Matt Damon, whose hero in the film *Good Will Hunting* tells his psychiatrist that *A People's History of the United States* will "knock you on your ass."

IS THERE SOMETHING WRONG WITH HISTORY PEOPLE WANT TO READ?

Flynn castigates Eric Foner, the *New York Times* book reviewer, for saying the book should be "required reading" for students. Noting that Amazon.com rated the book among the top sellers at major universities, Flynn wondered if the remarkable popularity of the book on college campuses was a result of "coercion" from teachers assigning the book to students.

Flynn calls Zinn's work "biased journalism," and to his way of thinking, there could be no better attack on Zinn's writing than to mark it with the dishonorable stain of bias. Flynn concludes, "This slanderous tome and its popular and academic success are monuments to human credulity and delusion, and to the disgraceful condition of American letters."

An interviewer from the *Boston Globe* asked Zinn if his writing was "fiercely partisan." Zinn explained, "Long before I decided to write *A People's History*, my partisanship was shaped by my upbringing in a working-class immigrant family, by my three years as a shipyard worker, by my experience as a bombardier in World War II, and by the civil rights movement in the South and the movement against the war in Vietnam. Educators and politicians may say that students ought to learn pure facts, innocent of interpretation, but there's no such thing! So I've chosen to emphasize voices of resistance—to class oppression, racial injustice, sexual inequality, nationalist arrogance—left out of the orthodox histories."

Zinn's view of history is passionate, personally involved. It is a people's history, told by a participant, not a cold dispassionate outside observer. Reading *A People's History of the United States* is a transformative experience, changing the way we understand and appreciate past events and culture.

6

Howard Zinn: A Life in History

In the world of Howard Zinn the subjects of history are intertwined with the lives of the ordinary people one encounters on the street during the course of a day. In his own life he has never separated the history he wrote about or taught in classrooms from the reality of his own existence and that of other people in the world. He does not take the stance of an objective historian who imagines himself to be standing outside of history, evaluating it dispassionately. On the contrary, he is driven by his passion, and his perspective on history is personal. For him life and history are one.

For Zinn, there is also no clear separation between the present and the past. History is an ongoing story. Zinn's version of history is a great adventure, more like a great novel than a dry textbook. As a history professor, he often turned to historical fiction instead of textbooks to bring history to life for his students. As William Faulkner put it, "the past is never dead; it isn't even past." Zinn drew a line through history connecting the struggles of people of the present with those of the past.

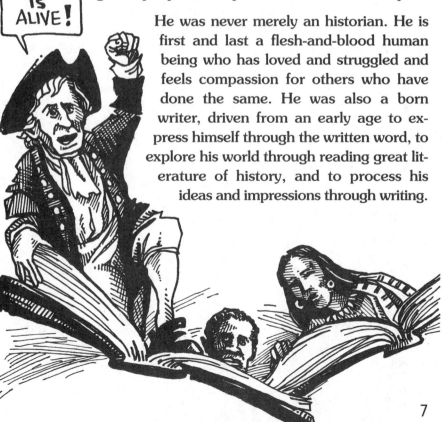

He was never merely an historian. He is first and last a flesh-and-blood human being who has loved and struggled and feels compassion for others who have done the same. He was also a born writer, driven from an early age to express himself through the written word, to explore his world through reading great literature of history, and to process his ideas and impressions through writing.

7

He was a teacher, who opened doors of the mind to thousands of students who passed through his classes. And he was an actor on the stage of history. Not merely a neutral bystander, he was an activist who dove into the struggles of his world and became one of the movers of history, who left a mark of his own, and encouraged others to do the same.

Zinn's life as an activist, his art as a writer, and his work as a teacher and historian are fused into one organic whole. By looking at his life, it is possible to develop an understanding of his ideas and his legacy as a historian. His life incorporates his history and vice versa.

Growing Up Working Class

Howard Zinn's story begins August 24, 1922, when he was born into a working class Jewish immigrant family on the Lower East Side of New York. He was the second of five boys born to Eddie and Jenny Zinn. Poverty was a nagging presence throughout his early life. His parents first met when they were both factory workers, and throughout their lives they worked hard just to keep the family housed and fed. Their first son died of spinal meningitis. Howard was stricken with rickets as a child, which made him skinny and frail. As a member of a poor family during the Depression, he had a working class consciousness from the beginning.

His father had come to America from Lemberg, a city in Eastern Europe that had at different times been part of the Austro-Hungarian empire, Poland, and the Soviet Union. Today it's known as the city of Lvov in the Ukraine. Howard's mother was from the Rabinowitz family of Irkutsk, Siberia, next to Lake Baikal near Mongolia. When people have commented on his Asiatic features, he has suggested, half seriously, that it may be because his ancestry traces back deep into Asia near Mongolia. Howard's parents were Jewish, he says, but neither of them was particularly religious.

Eddie Zinn worked various factory and labor jobs, as a window cleaner, pushcart peddler, necktie salesman, and WPA (Works Progress Administration) worker. He eventually settled into the dull drudgery of waiting tables at restaurants and weddings, and became a member of the waiters union. Young Howard sometimes worked with his father at New Year's Eve parties. He loathed it, especially the demeaning attitude of the bosses and customers toward the waiters.

Zinn's father never escaped poverty. "All his life he worked very hard for very little," Zinn wrote in his autobiography. "I've always resented the smug statements of politicians, media commentators, and corporate executives who talked of how, in America, if you worked hard you would become rich." The implication that if you were poor it was because you hadn't worked hard enough was a lie, to Howard. He had seen his father and many others who worked harder than big time businessmen or politicians, but Eddie Zinn and others among his class never escaped poverty despite their diligence.

A Child's Discovery of the Written Word

Zinn's inherent affinity for the written word expressed itself early, in spite of the odds against it. The Zinn family was deeply engaged in an intense struggle for survival, always moving from place to place, and there were no books in the Zinn home. But by the time Howard was eight, he had become a voracious reader, reading whatever he could get his hands on. The first book he owned was a copy of *Tarzan and the Jewels of Opar*, which he found on the street, minus some pages.

As poor as they were, his parents recognized his passion for books and tried to provide him with reading material whenever possible. With coupons saved from the *New York Post* every week Howard was able to buy one book a week for a few cents until he had acquired the entire collection of Charles Dickens' writings. Reading *David Copperfield, A Tale of Two Cities, Hard Times, Great Expectations,* and *Oliver Twist* greatly influenced his view of the world.

Dickens brought to life the oppression of the working classes, and Howard was deeply moved by the stories and the characters. In later years he expressed admiration for Dickens' technique of portraying class oppression from the standpoint of children. It brought to life dramatically the harsh injustice of a social system that virtually enslaved young children. Because victims of the system were often children, the stories undercut the standard argument that people who were poor were to blame for their condition.

In 2001 Zinn told Harry Kreisler of the Institute of International Studies, "From Dickens what I got was this ferocious acknowledgement of the modern industrial system and what it does to people, and how poor people live and the way they are victimized, and the way the courts function. The way justice works against the poor. Yes, it was Dickens's class consciousness that reinforced my own. It was a kind of justification for the beliefs I was already developing. Yes; it told me, what reading very often does for you, tells you are not alone in these secret thoughts you have."

Because his family moved so much, he changed schools often and got used to being the new kid in class. But in spite of the constant moving, he was such a good student that he was allowed to skip a grade when he transferred to Thomas Jefferson High School in Brooklyn, where he joined a writers program and a writers club.

His parents scraped together the money to buy him a typewriter and he taught himself how to type. He soon became as dedicated to writing as he was to reading. Writing became a constant activity, like a bodily function. Every time he read a book, he typed a review of it. But his family's persistent financial problems eventually became a distraction from studies and Howard became alienated from school. He started skipping classes, sometimes playing hooky for weeks at a time and devising schemes to elude the truant officer.

Writing

In 2008 Zinn reflected on his development as a writer:

I don't know if I considered myself a 'writer' consciously, but I did start to write almost as soon as I began to read, when I kept a notebook with reviews of the books I read. I was reading Upton Sinclair and John Steinbeck and Richard Wright and Charles Dickens. I was thirteen when my parents bought me a used Underwood #5 typewriter, which came with a booklet with instructions—showing the keyboard, etc. I just wrote reviews. But I saw myself as a journalist, and in the Air Force, coming back from overseas, stationed at Barksdale Field in Shreveport, Louisiana, I edited a newspaper called the Barksdale Bark for the airfield, and wrote some bold editorials criticizing the army for keeping soldiers in the service after the war was over. Of course as a student at NYU and a graduate student at Columbia, I was writing papers and a masters essay and a doctoral dissertation, and in all of those instances writing in a popular style, avoiding scholarly jargon. It was only when I went south and became involved in SNCC [Student Nonviolent Coordinating Committee]and the Southern movement that I started writing about what I saw in the South, as a participant in the movement, writing about the demonstrations in Albany, Georgia; Selma, Alabama; various towns in Mississippi. As for fiction, I spent a summer around 1959 writing a novel based on the Colorado mine strike of 1912-14 and the Ludlow Massacre, but it was rejected by several publishers and I dropped it. I only began writing plays—though I had long wanted to, my whole family being involved in the theater at one time or another—when the Vietnam War was over and I could stop speaking and writing about the war, with time now to work on a play. At this point I have no desire to write any more books. After writing a 700-page history book that has sold almost two million copies, and a number of other books, I feel I have said pretty much what I have wanted to say, though I still write short pieces, columns for The Progressive, articles for The Nation, op-ed pieces for the Boston Globe and other newspapers. If I get some time, I want to write another play. I'm not thinking of anything autobiographical. [Interview with the author]

Radicalization

Though his working class point of view was a natural result of growing up poor, Zinn pinpoints one particular moment that galvanized him politically and turned him into a radical. It was about 1940, at the beginning of World War II. Zinn was seventeen years old. He had become acquainted with some young people who were members of the Communist Party. Many socially conscious Americans at that time still thought Communism might be a positive movement that would undo some of the social injustices in the world.

In the early twentieth century, for example, the Communist Party was the only political party that supported voting rights for blacks in America. Communism had emerged as a more humane alternative to the predatory form of capitalism that had led to the Great Depression, in which millions were left poor and homeless in America. Americans who called themselves Communists in those days held to a more idealistic view of Communism than was actually being practiced by Stalin in Russia.

The young Communists Zinn met were intelligent and well-informed. Their arguments were persuasive. Though Zinn did not become a convert to their cause, he did accept an invitation to participate in a demonstration in Times Square in support for peace, justice, and similar causes. According to Zinn, the demonstration was proceeding in an orderly and nonviolent way, when suddenly he heard sirens and screaming. Hundreds of policemen charged into the crowd, some on horses and some on foot, swinging clubs into people's heads. One police officer's swinging club caught Zinn on the skull and he was knocked unconscious. When he came to, with an aching lump on his head, the world looked different.

Zinn was profoundly shocked that such a thing could happen in America. Wasn't America a democracy where people had the right to speak, write, assemble, and demonstrate to express their grievances, as guaranteed by the Constitution and the Bill of Rights? In one swift blow, his faith in democracy, equality, and freedom of the individual in America were shattered. Suddenly he saw that the Communists were right. The police weren't impartial peace-keepers, enforcing the law and the Constitution equally and fairly for all people. They were servants of the rich and powerful. Free speech was a fine thing in the high-flown words of the Constitution. But if you offended the established powers by saying the wrong things, you might well end up on the wrong side of a club or a gun, or under the galloping hooves of a horse.

That crash on the skull changed Zinn's perspective on the world. Up until then, he had considered himself a liberal who believed in American democracy and its ability to correct itself as it progressed along the twists and turns of history. But no more. From then on, he was a radical. Now he felt strongly that something was terribly wrong with the system, and that the illness was deeper than he had previously believed. It would not be cured by merely electing a new president or passing some new legislation. Fixing the problem would require tearing down the old order to its foundation, and rebuilding a society based on equality, peace, and cooperation.

Love and War

After Zinn graduated from Thomas Jefferson High School he enrolled in Brooklyn College. Attendance was free, but Howard's family's economic problems were so severe that he still couldn't afford to go to school. There was no time for education; he needed to produce an income. So at age eighteen, he dropped out of college and went to work in a shipyard. For three years he worked on the docks, building battleships for the war and helping to land ships. Working in freezing cold and stifling heat, Zinn felt the hardships of his labor: His ears were pummeled by deafening noises while his lungs and sinuses were invaded by poisonous fumes.

But harsh as conditions were, Howard's time in the shipyard brought him to his most sublime, transcendent experience, his meeting with the love of his life, Roslyn Schechter in 1942. It started, however, on a note of betrayal.

A basketball buddy of Howard's asked him to deliver his army insignia to a girl he had a crush on but was too shy to approach himself. Howard tracked Roslyn down at her parents' apartment, and when he encountered her, he was smitten. Roslyn had beautiful, long, chestnut blonde hair and the face of a Russian beauty in Howard's estimation. He was delighted when she suggested they take a walk around the block.

Roz and Howard found an instant affinity. Roslyn shared Howard's passion for reading. In fact, his Russian beauty was deeply absorbed in the works of Dostoevsky and Tolstoy. He was immersed in the works of Marx and Engels and the fiction of Upton Sinclair. They had similar attitudes and feelings about the most urgent issues and controversies of the time, such as socialism, fascism, and World War II.

Meeting Roslyn galvanized him, awakened new horizons and aspirations. After living his life in a grim working class netherworld, and running into a dead end after high school, Howard felt the intense desire to shake things up. He and Roz were both passionately anti-fascist and saw World War II as a battle against tyranny, racial discrimination, militarism, fanatic nationalism, and expansionism. He wanted to be a part of the struggle, so he volunteered for the Army Air Corps.

Without even telling his parents, he walked into the induction center and volunteered. He was subjected to a battery of physical and mental tests, and then was told he had been rejected. But the fiery young Howard was not to be deterred. His desire to fight fascism was so fervent, he asked to see the examining officer again, and pleaded to be allowed to join the fight. The officer was so impressed with Zinn's zeal that he relented and let him join.

His induction ushered in a period of intense movement around the United States in preparation for war. It began with four months of basic training as an infantryman at Jefferson Barracks, Missouri, where he was indoctrinated in the fundamental skills and attitudes of soldiering. He was then transferred to Burlington, Vermont, where he learned how to fly a Piper Cub airplane. From there, he was whisked away to Nashville, Tennessee, to take exams to determine whether he would be better suited to serve as a pilot, a navigator, or a bombardier. When it was decided that he would be a bombardier, he was sent on to Santa Ana, California, for preflight training, to Las Vegas for six weeks at gunnery school, and finally to Deming, New Mexico, to learn how to use the Norden bombsight. He had a good eye and was promoted to the rank of second lieutenant. By then he had earned his first furlough, eleven days at home before shipping off to Europe to begin bombing missions.

While he was in basic training, he and Roz got into an intense correspondence, developing an intimate relationship through letters. His passion for writing merged with his new love for Roslyn.

Howard poured out his thoughts, feelings, and experiences to her day by day for sixteen months. When he took his first furlough he went straight to see her. Four days later, on October 30, 1944, they were married in a ceremony attended only by parents and siblings. They spent a week-long honeymoon in a cheap Manhattan hotel, and then Howard had to take off again, this time for

Rapid City, South Dakota, where he was scheduled to meet his crew. Roslyn was allowed to join him there before he shipped off.

By then the Allied invasion of Europe was well underway. Howard was anxious to join the fight, and Roz shared his zeal. He changed places with other bombardiers twice in order to get moved up in line and shipped out earlier.

Doubts about War

During the very intense two-and-a-half year period in the army from May 1943 to December 1945, Zinn's idealism about "the Good War" was chipped away bit by bit. By the end of the war, he no longer believed that war solved problems at all. Several particular experiences mark his progression from an avid sup-porter of the war to a disillusioned warrior.

The first of the transformative experiences took place even before he reached the front, while heading to Europe on the Queen Mary. A random disruption in protocol led to a black man being acci-dentally seated next to a white sergeant in the eating area. The white sergeant flew into a rage and yelled, "Get him out of here till I finish!" Zinn was in charge of maintaining order in the mess hall and told the sergeant that if he objected to the conditions he was free to leave without finishing his food. "What is this war about anyway?" he added angrily and began to wonder himself.

Zinn learned a lesson from the bigoted sergeant that came in handy later during the civil rights struggles. Most racists have something they care about more than segregation. Figuring out what it was could be helpful when negotiating.

Impassioned as he was to fight fascism, he didn't take well to military order. He chafed against the strict class hierarchy and regimentation of military life. He and his buddies in his nine-man crew agreed to drop the salutes and the "yes-sirs" and "no-sirs" when they were among themselves. But on board ship, they had to comply with army protocol and the enlisted men had to eat separate from the officers.

Bombing Missions

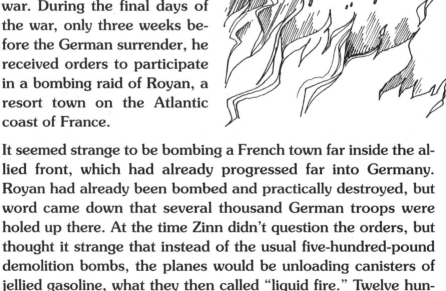

Zinn was stationed at East Anglia, England, flying bombing missions over Berlin, Czechoslovakia, and Hungary. One specific bombing mission had a particularly jolting effect on him, one that would contribute to his change of heart about war. During the final days of the war, only three weeks before the German surrender, he received orders to participate in a bombing raid of Royan, a resort town on the Atlantic coast of France.

It seemed strange to be bombing a French town far inside the allied front, which had already progressed far into Germany. Royan had already been bombed and practically destroyed, but word came down that several thousand German troops were holed up there. At the time Zinn didn't question the orders, but thought it strange that instead of the usual five-hundred-pound demolition bombs, the planes would be unloading canisters of jellied gasoline, what they then called "liquid fire." Twelve hundred bombers dumped napalm supposedly on German soldiers, but also on the French population. It was one of the first times napalm was used in warfare.

It was only much later that the full implications of what he had been doing as a bombardier dawned on him. From his vantage point high in the sky, all he could see of the bombs he dropped were flashes of light like matchsticks. He couldn't see people scorched and shattered, torn limb from limb. He couldn't hear their screams. He was just following orders. When he thought back on it later, it was clear that the Royan operation could not have had any significant effect on the military objectives of the war. Were they just testing a new weapon?

But that didn't occur to him when caught up in the fog of war. There was only one time during the war when he questioned the war's justification. A gunner he had become friends with one day told Zinn that they were not fighting a war against fascism. On the contrary, he said, it was a struggle among powerful empires for dominance over the resources of the world. Great Britain, the United States, the Soviet Union—they were all corrupt states. They had no moral qualms with Hitler's tyranny, violence, or racism. They just wanted to run the world themselves.

Zinn asked the gunner why he was there, and the answer was, "To talk to guys like you." Zinn was struck and couldn't get it out of his mind. When he returned from the war, he gathered his war memorabilia into an envelope, wrote "never again" on it, and stashed it away out of sight.

Hiroshima and Questions

Soon after war in Europe ended, Zinn heard the news of the atomic bombs dropped on Hiroshima and Nagasaki, followed by news that the war was over and massive, ecstatic celebrations and euphoria in the streets. Like everyone else, Zinn was happy that the war was over. No one had any idea what an atomic bomb was. They just knew that the fighting was done and it was cause for celebration. The evil fascists had been defeated.

After the war Zinn read John Hersey's book *Hiroshima*, which vividly portrayed the hell created by the atomic bomb for the people of Hiroshima. Through Hersey, he was transported to the scene of the horror, seeing people with their skin burned and hanging from their bodies, their eyeballs pushed out of their sockets, arms and legs torn off, atrocious wounds, and radioactive poisoning in their blood. Much later, as a fellow at Harvard's Center for East Asian studies, he studied the bombing more and published an article called "A Mess of Death and Documents." He learned from interviews with seven hundred Japanese officers that they had been on the verge of surrender before the bombs were dropped on Hiroshima and Nagasaki. They would have certainly surrendered within a few months, without the bombings and without an invasion of Japan. Zinn came to believe that the bomb had been dropped for strategic motives, to beat Japan before the Russians could, and to demonstrate America's military prowess to the Soviets. The last act of World War II was the first act of the Cold War.

22

Through his experience over Royan he came to believe that military development creates its own momentum, often overtaking the human concerns and the original intentions of those who choose to go to war. Military establishments do not want to waste a newly developed weapon. The military machine wants to test its new weapons, exercise its might.

Years later, in August of 1966, Howard and Roz were invited to Hiroshima by a Japanese peace group to commemorate the anniversary of the dropping on the bomb. Howard was asked to speak at a community center for survivors of the bomb. When he looked out upon his audience, many of them tragically disfigured from the bomb, he couldn't speak.

Final Blows of War

The final blows to Zinn's belief in the justifications for the war came when he lost his two closest army buddies in the very last weeks of the war. Ed Plotkin was twenty-six; Joe Perry was only nineteen. A few days after the war in Europe was declared over, Zinn received a letter he had sent to Joe Perry, returned marked "Deceased."

When he returned to New York he looked up Ed Plotkin. He found out from Plotkin's wife that her husband had been killed in a plane crash over the Pacific only a few days before the war was over. In a strange twist of fate, Plotkin had snuck out from Fort Dix for one final rendezvous with his wife before being shipped off to war, and in that meeting they had conceived a child. Ed Plotkin would never know he had a daughter.

Many years later when Professor Zinn was teaching, he received a note saying, "Ed Plotkin's daughter wants to meet you." He spent time with her and told her everything he could remember about the father who was taken before she would ever see him.

The loss of his two best army buddies left a bitter sting and a marked change to his approach to life. "I feel I have been given a gift–undeserved, just luck–almost fifty years of life," he wrote in his memoir. "I am always aware of that." Often Ed and Joe would appear in a recurring dream, reminding him of his great fortune, the gift of life. He would wake up with renewed commitment to living life fully, not wasting it, and trying to give something back. He felt he owed it to Ed and Joe to try to make whatever effort he could to try to realize the dream of the better world that they all believed they were fighting for.

The memory of Ed and Joe provided a compass to remind him he had no right to sink into despair. He must insist on hope that a better world is possible. And it was Ed and Joe, more than anything, who brought home to him the reality of war, the suffering of those so far below him as he unloaded bombs from the sky. The war was over, but nagging doubts took hold inside him. Was it all really necessary?

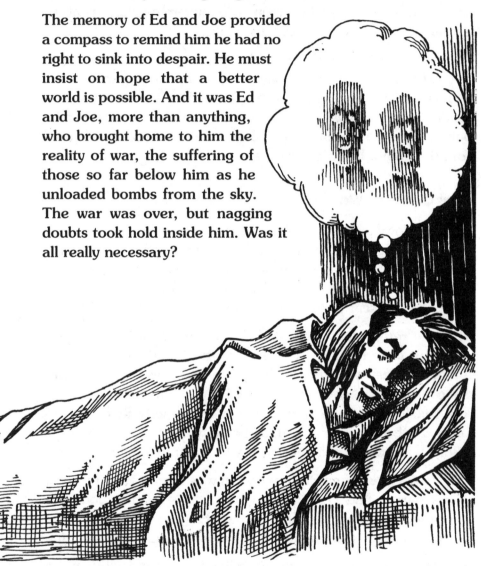

The Nazis were so evil that opposing them seemed the only decent, just thing to do. The war was seen almost universally as a "good war." But as he reflected on it, Zinn came to the conclusion that once war is in progress; the whole process is so degrading to human morality that it begins to make both sides look increasingly alike in their barbaric brutality. As in Royan, the good guys often bombed people who were supposedly "on our side." The brutality of allied bombings of innocent civilians in both Germany and Japan was overall much worse than the "bad guys" had done in the first place.

If the allied governments were really, as they claimed, going to war against the evils of fascism, why did they stand by and do nothing when Japan was slaughtering innocent Chinese civilians, or when General Franco, with Hitler's help, was bombing his own countrymen in Spain? (Franco remained in power for decades after the war.) And though the Americans opposed the crimes against humanity of the Nazis, at home the U.S. government put Japanese Americans into concentration camps and maintained a system of violent oppression of African Americans held over from the days of slavery.

War, he concluded, is not some deeply embedded need of human beings; it is manipulated by political leaders, who use propaganda and coercion to force people to participate. Without that, the public is not interested in war. In 1917 the U.S. government sent seventy-five thousand lecturers around the country to give lectures to millions of people to stir up support for World War I. In later times the propaganda was broadcast through mass media to millions of people.

In 2005 Zinn told Amy Goodman of *Democracy Now,* "In modern warfare, soldiers fire, they drop bombs, and they have no notion, really, of what is happening to the human beings that they're firing on. Everything is done at a distance. This enables terrible atrocities to take place. And I think reflecting back on that bombing raid, and thinking of that in Hiroshima and all of the other raids on civilian cities and the killing of huge numbers of civilians in German and Japanese cities, the killing of a hundred thousand people in Tokyo in one night of fire-bombing—all of that made me realize war, even so-called good wars against fascism like World War II, wars don't solve any fundamental problems, and they always poison everybody on both sides. They poison the minds and souls of everybody on both sides. We are seeing that now in Iraq, where the minds of our soldiers are being poisoned by being an occupying army in a land where they are not wanted. And the results are terrible."

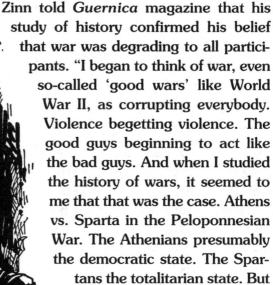

Zinn told *Guernica* magazine that his study of history confirmed his belief that war was degrading to all participants. "I began to think of war, even so-called 'good wars' like World War II, as corrupting everybody. Violence begetting violence. The good guys beginning to act like the bad guys. And when I studied the history of wars, it seemed to me that that was the case. Athens vs. Sparta in the Peloponnesian War. The Athenians presumably the democratic state. The Spartans the totalitarian state. But as the war went on—and you can see this in Thucydides's History of the Peloponnesian War—the Athenians began to act like the Spartans. They began committing atrocities and cruelties. So I saw this as a characteristic of war, even so-called 'good wars.'"

Back to School

Back home from the war, Zinn wanted to further his education. Fortunately at that time, the GI Bill would pay his fees. But even with the government paying his tuition, Zinn could not at first afford to go to school. Man cannot live by education alone. He must have food and shelter. He must have income.

For a while, Howard and Roz tried living with Roz' parents, but that didn't work. To break out on their own, they had to establish a home and an economic base. Roz got a job as a secretary and Howard tried going back to work at the shipyard. He went through a series of depressing, dead-end jobs that included waiting tables, digging ditches, and working in a brewery. Between jobs he collected unemployment insurance.

Howard and Roz managed to rent a rat-infested basement apartment in Bedford Stuyvesant, Brooklyn, a notoriously tough neighborhood. Soon after, their first child, a daughter they named Myla, was born. And then, in 1949, three years after leaving the military and with his second child on the way, Howard, at age twenty-seven, returned to school as a freshman at New York University.

Though the GI Bill paid the tuition, Howard still had to work full-time to make ends meet. He attended classes during the day and worked from 4 p.m. to midnight at a Manhattan warehouse loading trucks. Roz also worked part time. Soon the family got a place the on the Lower East Side of Manhattan in a low-income housing project near the East River. It was a big improvement. It had no ants or cockroaches. It even had some trees and a playground on the grounds of the project.

The Graduate

Zinn burned through the undergraduate requirements at NYU in only two and a half years. In 1951, he graduated with a bachelor's degree. He enrolled at Columbia University for graduate school, majoring in history with a minor in economics. He became fascinated with the history of labor struggles and wrote his master's thesis about the Colorado coal strike of 1913-1914. The thesis reappeared much later in the form of an essay called "The Ludlow Massacre" in his book *The Politics of History,* published in 1970. In 1952 he received his master's degree from Columbia.

Zinn told *Revolutionary Worker* in 1998, "I got into history not to be a historian, not to be a scholar, not to be an academic, not to write scholarly articles for scholarly journals, not to go to academic conferences to deliver papers to bored fellow historians. I got into history because I was already an activist at the age of eighteen. I was working in a shipyard. I was organizing young shipyard workers. And I was introduced to radical ideas. I was reading Marx, I was reading Upton Sinclair, I was reading Jack London, I was reading *The Grapes of Wrath.* So I was a politically aware young man working in the shipyard. I was there for three years. Then I enlisted in the Air Force. I was a bombardier in the United States Air Force, and came out and worked at various jobs. All of these influences: I came from a working class family… my upbringing."

After earning his master's, he went on for his doctoral degree, again majoring in history but this time with a minor in political science. While at Columbia he studied with some of the most respected historians of the time, including Richard Hofstadter, Henry Steele Commager, David Donald, Richard Morris, Jacques Barzun, and William Leuchtenburg.

Though Zinn didn't actually take any courses from Hofstadter, Hoftstadter did chair his dissertation defense. Zinn was impressed with Hofstadter's writing, particularly an early work, *The American Political Tradition,* which reflected Hofstadter's younger, more radical inclinations.

Zinn also admired Professor David Donald for his deep personal involvement in his teaching. For him history was not just an abstract, academic study, but something living, something that really moved him. Zinn was impressed when he watched Donald give a lecture on the abolitionists with tears in his eyes. That was the way any subject should be taught, Zinn thought. Teachers should teach about things about which they are truly passionate.

A Teaching Job

Zinn's teaching career began with a back injury while working at the warehouse, after which he was forced to look for an alternative to a job with heavy lifting. He managed to get hired for two part-time teaching jobs. Zinn found that part-time teachers often end up doing more work than full time professors. He taught two evening courses at Brooklyn College and four day courses at Upsala College in East Orange, New Jersey. He had to drive an hour west into New Jersey four days each week and an hour east to Brooklyn on the two other days, alternating back and forth between a daytime schedule and a nighttime schedule. Upsala needed teachers for government more than for history, so his minor in political science came in handy.

Even before he received his doctoral degree, Zinn was offered an interview with the visiting president of Spelman College, a school for African American women in Atlanta, Georgia, during which he was offered a position heading the college's small history and social science department. It was a chance to pull himself out of the commuting routine and take a full-time job as a tenured professor. He took the offer, even though it meant moving his family to Atlanta. It was 1956.

The civil rights movement that was to blossom in the 1960s was still just a glimmer in 1956. The Supreme Court decision Brown versus the Board of Education of Topeka had been issued in 1954. It declared that the fourteenth amendment to the Constitution prohibited racial segregation in schools, overturning earlier rulings that authorized "separate but equal" school facilities for blacks. But the decision had not done much to change the institutionalized racism of the U.S., especially in the South.

During the election of 1956, neither the incumbent President Eisenhower nor his Democratic Party challenger, Illinois Governor Adlai Stevenson, took a stand on civil rights. After the election, Eisenhower proposed the Civil Rights Act of 1957, and Republican congressmen, in an effort to win black votes, pushed it through, setting the stage for further action on civil rights. The U.S. was still in the grip of McCarthyism. Anti-Communist hysteria sent a cold chill of fear through all levels of society and pushed many entertainers, union activists, and educators out of work under suspicion of having Communist sympathies.

Out of the Blue

It had never occurred to Zinn that he might move his family down south or take a job teaching in a black college. On the other hand, some of his experiences had laid the groundwork for understanding the conditions under which black Americans lived. Living in the housing project in New York, he mixed constantly with people of all kinds of ethnic groups, including Irish Americans, Italian Americans, African Americans, and Puerto Rican Americans. In New York various races and nationalities lived side by side in integrated neighborhoods and apartment buildings. That didn't mean New York lacked racial prejudice. Zinn had seen plenty of prejudice on the basis of race as well as class.

His education in history had made only too clear the contradictions between the theory and practice of American democracy. The literature he read, including Richard Wright's *Native Son*, the poetry of Langston Hughes, and Upton Sinclair's *The Jungle*, had given him some insight into the conditions of being poor and black. While working as a laborer he had seen discrimination as blacks were excluded from labor unions and denied the opportunity to work. In the military he had seen racial prejudice institutionalized. And his own struggles as a member of a poor immigrant family had given him sympathy for others on the lower rungs of a tough, competitive society.

In his autobiography he wrote, "That was my world for the first thirty-three years of my life–the world of unemployment and bad employment, of me and my wife leaving our two- and three-year-olds in the care of others while we went to school or to work, living most of that time in cramped and unpleasant places, hesitating to call the doctor when the children were sick because we couldn't afford to pay him, finally taking the children to hospital clinics where interns could take care of them. This is the way a large part of the population lives, even in this, the richest country in the world. And when, armed with the proper degrees, I began to move out of that world, becoming a college professor, I never forgot that."

And yet, though he had not planned it, there was also a mark of destiny on his being suddenly transported from New York to Atlanta, in the heart of the segregated south, the home of Martin Luther King, Jr., a place that would emerge during Zinn's years there as a vital center of an historic civil rights struggle. Zinn settled down right in the middle of it. He was to become not only an eyewitness to some of the most intense transitions of American history, but he was also to be an active participant.

North to South

The Zinn family had to pack up, uproot, and leave New York, then transplant themselves in Atlanta, Georgia, which was in the '50s still deeply set in the traditions of white supremacy, with laws enforcing separation, or segregation, of the races. In a place where segregation had been the law of the land, white landlords were not enthusiastic about renting their properties to a professor at a school for black women, what they called the "nigra college." When he told them where he worked, he would find that there were no vacancies. Eventually, however, the Zinn family managed to find a small house in a friendly, white, working class neighborhood in the city of Decatur, east of Atlanta.

Atlanta was as segregated in 1956 as Johannesburg, South Africa, Zinn said. If a black person was seen downtown it was because he or she was working for a white person. And if a black and white person appeared together, and it wasn't clearly demonstrated that the black was working for the white, the ambiance of the area would suddenly become very tense. The students of Spelman, being both black and female, felt that they had two strikes against them. Getting a good education was one way to try to compensate for that fact. A college degree was a way to arm themselves to face a cold, harsh world that was indifferent to their aspirations as human beings.

As a northerner plunged into southern segregation, Zinn was suddenly confronted with the rude reality of the segregated south. He soon penetrated the polite decorum of his students and perceived it as a cover for the lifetime of indignation they harbored for being treated like second class human beings, or animals. Once he asked his students to write down their first memory of racial prejudice, and it opened the floodgates to their feelings of being discriminated against since birth.

As a teacher, Zinn believed in total involvement. The commonly held belief that professional people should not mix their personal or political beliefs with their work made no sense to him. He saw no reason why a teacher or a historian should have to separate his profession from his own personal concerns and convictions. In the course of his profession, he found himself on a collision course with the old class hierarchy of the South.

Challenging the System

A few months after starting his job, he took a group of students to observe a session of the Georgia State Legislator. As they looked for a place to sit, they found themselves facing a sign that said "colored." It was a proclamation that ordered African Americans to confine themselves to that part of the gallery. The general seating area, however, was practically empty, so the students decided to sit there.

The venerable congressmen, engaged in a serious discussion about fishing rights, were suddenly no longer able to carry on their business, so unnerved were they by the sight of the black women in the white section. The Speaker of the House exploded into a rage, grabbed the microphone, and ordered the "nigras" to get back where they belonged. The congressional floor practically broke into a riot as the legislators joined the chorus of angry yells at the students who were defying their sacred institutions of white supremacy. The police were called to the scene, and the students backed down and chose to submit to sitting in the colored section; it was a better alternative than going to jail, getting kicked out of college, or being cut off from their opportunity for an education.

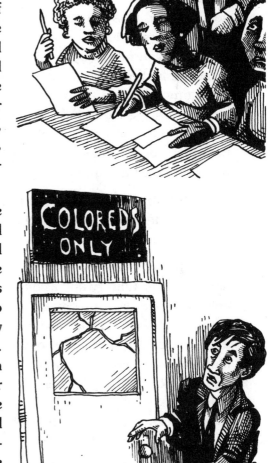

As the students filed into the colored section and Zinn stood nearby, a guard approached him. Zinn explained that the young women were students from Spelman College who had come to learn about how the legislature was conducted. The guard disappeared and a few minutes later the Speaker of the House approached the podium again and addressed the gallery. This time his manner had changed to a grandiose display of magnanimity as he welcomed the Spelman students to the session.

As the faculty sponsor of the Social Science Club, Zinn frequently took his students on field trips and undertook projects with them. Early in 1959, Zinn suggested to the students of the club that they take on a project involving social change. One student came up with an idea for confronting the policies of racism in the public libraries.

Despite the 1954 Supreme Court ruling that outlawed segregation in schools and public facilities, the southern institutions of racial discrimination remained solidly entrenched. The Brown versus Board of Education decision established integration as the federal law, overruling any local laws to the contrary. The federal government was theoretically obligated to enforce the law against segregation, but the change was not so easy to enforce. If people wanted the system to change, they would have to confront the institutions of racism and the people who maintained them one by one. In a confrontation, the federal law was theoretically on the side of the challengers. But centuries of inertia were on the side of the old ways. And hate, fear, and viciousness were deeply tied up in maintaining the old system of oppression that had grown out of centuries of slavery.

Though public libraries could not legally be segregated, blacks were routinely sent away from all of the Atlanta libraries except those designated specifically for blacks.

Black students began to initiate change by going into the whites-only Carnegie Library and asking for classic works on freedom and equality, such as John Stuart Mill's *On Liberty,* Thomas Paine's *Common Sense,* or the Declaration of Independence. They knew they would be turned away and directed to the black library. But librarians were educated people and it was disturbing for them to be reminded of the contradiction between the principles underlying the creation of the United States and their practice of turning away blacks. The students increased the frequency of their requests, then alerted the librarians that they were considering filing a lawsuit. The Library Board met in a panic and finally settled on ending its policy on segregation.

It was a small
victory, not one of the dramatic
moments usually singled out by historians. But according to Zinn, though his-
tory tends to focus on major milestones, it is not just those major
moments that bring about social change, but a multitude of small
actions that prepare the way for large breakthrough events.

Zinn became increasingly involved in the struggles, participating
in many demonstrations, picketing, and marching against segregation in many places. During that period he was only arrested
once, and ironically it was not at a demonstration. On a cold
night in 1959, he was driving and came upon one of his students,
Roslyn Pope, an honor student who just returned from a scholarship year in Paris. He offered Roslyn a lift to her dorm. When
they arrived, Zinn stopped the car, and they spoke a few
moments more before Roslyn pre-
pared to get out of the car.
Suddenly they found
themselves in

the glare of police car lights and a police officer ordered them out of the car. Zinn asked the officer what the charge was. "You're sittin' in a car with a nigger gal and wantin' to know what's the charge?" the officer answered. The police took them to the station, booked them for disorderly conduct, and took them into custody.

Zinn asked to make the one phone call he was allowed and he was pointed to a pay phone, which was useless to him since he had no change. Fortunately another prisoner gave him a dime, but he then discovered the wire to the telephone had been cut. Not to be deterred, he held the ends of the severed wire together while he called a lawyer, who came and got Zinn and the student released before dawn. Zinn felt like he was living through a story by Franz Kafka.

By early 1960 Roslyn Pope was class president at Spelman. As demonstrations gained momentum across the South, students from the five black colleges connected with Atlanta University (Morehouse College, Clark, Morris Brown, the Theological Center, and Spelman) began making plans to stage actions to take on segregation in Atlanta. Julian Bond, a Morehouse student who later became famous as an activist and a member of the Georgia House of Representatives, and Lonnie King, a football star, contacted students from the other black colleges to join forces and coordinate efforts. Word of their plans reached the presidents of the colleges, who began scrambling for a way to divert a confrontation.

The presidents proposed an alternative to demonstrations. They suggested that the students address their grievances by running a full-page ad in the *Atlanta Constitution*, for which the college presidents offered to raise the money. The students accepted the offer, and Roslyn Pope was designated to write the ad, but the presidents had achieved only a slight reprieve. Their problems were not over.

The ad appeared in the *Constitution* under the title "An Appeal for Human Rights." The presidents were not prepared for the soaring rhetoric of Ms. Pope. The ad said that the students had joined their hearts, minds, and bodies to gain the rights for which the Declaration of Independence said they were entitled as human beings. And furthermore, it said, echoing the Declaration of Independence, "We do not intend to wait placidly for those rights which are already legally and morally ours to be meted out to us one at a time." In fact, the ad said, the students intended to "use every legal and nonviolent means" to secure the rights of full citizenship. The ad set off a firestorm of anger and indignation that spread rapidly from the college presidents all the way up to Georgia Governor Ernest Vandiver, who issued a statement calling the ad "anti-American," saying it was "obviously not written by a student," and in fact, did not "sound like it was written in this country."

This was not long after Senator Joseph McCarthy's anti-Communism hearings, when lives were destroyed by accusations of Communist sympathies. The Red Scare had waned a bit, but hatred of Communism was still a handy device for discrediting anything that might be threatening to the establishment. Vandiver's claim that the ad sounded like it was not written in America was a veiled accusation that the students were being encouraged and influenced by foreign Communists.

But the threat failed to intimidate the students. In fact, his troubles were about to get much worse. A few days after the ad appeared hundreds of black students staged sit-ins at ten different cafeterias in downtown Atlanta. In synchronization at 11 a.m., hundreds of students took forbidden whites-only seats in restaurants, and when they were ordered to leave, they refused.

Seventy-seven demonstrators were arrested, including fourteen Spelman students. They were charged with multiple counts of conspiracy, breaching the peace, intimidating restaurant owners, and refusing to leave the premises, charges that could have earned each one of them up to ninety years in prison. But with so many cases, the system was overwhelmed and the students were never brought to trial. One of the Spelman students was Marian Wright, who would later become famous as the first black woman lawyer in Mississippi and the founder of the Children's Defense Fund.

At one of the 1960 demonstrations Howard and Roslyn Zinn participated by sitting down for coffee with two black students at the segregated lunch counter of Rich's Department Store in Atlanta. When the management asked them to leave, they refused. The management didn't want to call the police, cause a scene, and draw attention to the store's policy of segregation, which was increasingly an embarrassment. On the other hand, letting blacks sit with whites at the lunch counter blatantly defied centuries of ingrained habits and offended some customers. In frustration and confusion, they decided to just close the store. They

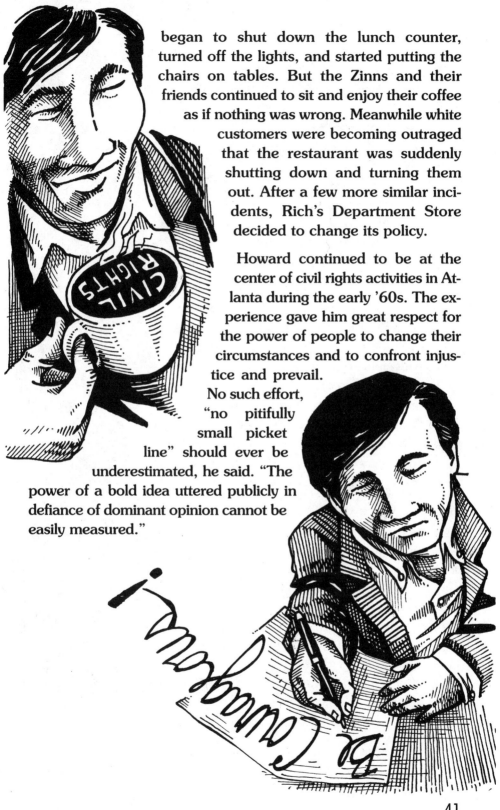

began to shut down the lunch counter, turned off the lights, and started putting the chairs on tables. But the Zinns and their friends continued to sit and enjoy their coffee as if nothing was wrong. Meanwhile white customers were becoming outraged that the restaurant was suddenly shutting down and turning them out. After a few more similar incidents, Rich's Department Store decided to change its policy.

Howard continued to be at the center of civil rights activities in Atlanta during the early '60s. The experience gave him great respect for the power of people to change their circumstances and to confront injustice and prevail. No such effort, "no pitifully small picket line" should ever be underestimated, he said. "The power of a bold idea uttered publicly in defiance of dominant opinion cannot be easily measured."

Expelled

Zinn's activism finally, perhaps inevitably, got him fired from Spelman. The specific events leading to his dismissal began in spring of 1963 when one of his students, Herschelle Sullivan, wrote an editorial for the college paper complaining about Spelman's tight control over its students, specifically referring to the administration's relationship with students as "benevolent despotism."

Spelman's president, Dr. Albert Manley, was enraged at being referred to by implication as a tyrant. As the college's first black president, Manley was in a tight spot. He could easily become a scapegoat for the white establishment over the rise of activism and rebelliousness during his term as president. Manley panicked and began to take steps to restore order. But significant events were changing the old South.

Manley threw a tirade against Sullivan for writing the article and against the editors of the paper for publishing it. Zinn rose to Sullivan's defense and wrote Manley a long letter saying that he had encouraged students in his classes to think independently and to be courageous in the face of repression. He further asserted that the administration's effort to discourage freedom of expression was a violation of the values of a liberal arts education. Manley responded with cold silence. Five other faculty members wrote similar letters to Zinn's. Manley still did not respond. Tensions mounted.

Students presented a petition to the administration asking it to promote a new atmosphere that would better prepare students for the "rapidly changing world." Furious that others would question his mission, Manley told student leaders that if they didn't like Spelman, they could leave. He demanded that the school newspaper pull the petition from the paper before it went to press. The honors student who helped publicize the petition received a letter notifying her that her application for a scholarship had been denied on the basis of poor citizenship.

In response, the students invited the faculty to a meeting to discuss these issues. A dozen teachers came, but not Manley. Later, at a faculty meeting chaired by Manley, Zinn suggested listening to a tape of the students' meeting to hear their grievances, but Manley refused. Zinn visited Manley in his office to smooth over the tensions. But Manley was unmoved. He saw Zinn as an instigator and believed the students would not take such actions without someone older putting them up to it.

Two months later, when the semester was over, and Zinn and his family were packing up to drive north for the summer, Zinn received a letter from Manley telling him his appointment would not be renewed. Zinn was tenured and had some rights, but fighting the decision through the courts would have been difficult, expensive, and time consuming. He was given one year's pay to discourage him from taking action. He took the extra year's salary and moved on. His acquiescence earned him a year to concentrate on his writing. Years later, the American Association of University Professors would investigate the incident and cite Spelman for violating Zinn's academic freedom.

Howard Zinn and Alice Walker

One of the most valuable and enduring legacies of Zinn's tenure at Spelman was a friendship he developed with one of this students, Alice Walker, who later became the Pulitzer Prize winning author of *The Color Purple, In Love and Trouble,* and many other popular books of fiction and poetry, as well as biographies and essays. When she arrived at Spelman she was fresh off her family's farm in Eatontown, Georgia.

Zinn met Walker when he happened to be seated next to her at an honors dinner for freshmen. They hit it off immediately and became friends for life. She enrolled in his Russian history course, where he had students read from great works of Russian literature by Gogol, Chekhov, Dostoevsky, and Tolstoy. Zinn first became aware of Walker's prowess as a writer when she turned in an essay on Dostoevsky and Tolstoy that stunned him. He said he had rarely read a literary essay "of such grace and style" by anyone.

When Walker came to Spelman, the civil rights demonstrations had already been going on for a while, and she soon became part of the action. She became a frequent visitor at the Zinn home. Soon after he was fired from Spelman, Walker also left, writing a sad farewell letter to him that said, "There is nothing really here for me."

About Zinn, Walker wrote, "What can I say that will in any way convey the love, respect, and admiration I feel for this unassuming hero who was my teacher and mentor, this radical historian and people-loving 'trouble-maker,' this man who stood with us and suffered with us? Howard Zinn was the best teacher I ever had, and the funniest. Here is a history teacher and a history maker to give us hope, especially the young, for whom he has always committed so much of his life."

SNCC

Zinn's relationship as an advisor to the Student Nonviolent Coordinating Committee (SNCC) began soon after its founding in 1960 when students who had participated in sit-ins formed the organization on the campus of Shaw University in Raleigh, North Carolina. The students of SNCC asked Zinn to be one of two adult advisers and to join their executive committee. He became increasingly involved in the civil rights struggle as it intensified.

In summer of 1962 Zinn took on a research project for a liberal research group in Atlanta called the Southern Regional Council. He was asked to look into racial conflict that had been spiraling out of control over the last several months in the town of Albany, Georgia. A white civil rights activist named Bill Hansen was arrested with sixteen other people and put into a cell with a white prisoner, who was told that Hansen was one of those meddling northerners who had come down south "to straighten us out." It was an implicit license to enact violence and the prisoner took the hint. While Hansen sat on the floor of the cell reading a newspaper, his cellmate attacked him, knocked him unconscious, and beat him, leaving him with a split lip, a broken jaw, and fractured ribs. When a young black attorney named C.B. King walked into the sheriff's office that afternoon to inquire about what happened to Hansen, he got a taste of Albany justice. The sheriff smashed his nightstick against King's head. King stumbled out of the

45

office, reeling, with blood streaming down his face, and staggered across the street to the office of police chief Laurie Pritchett, who called for medical aid.

Sheriff Cull Campbell of Daugherty County in Albany, Georgia, was deeply entrenched in the nastiest racism ever produced by Southern culture. He did not mask his racial bigotry and hatred with a pretense of gentility. He resorted to deadly violence in the blink of an eye. It was a bold move to even walk into his office, as Zinn did a few weeks later, to inquire about the incidents with Hansen and King.

When Zinn walked into the sheriff's headquarters and asked to see him, Campbell invited him back into his office, then turned, stared him in the face and said, "You're not with the goddamn niggers are you?" Zinn just asked what had happened to King. Campbell said, "Yeah, I knocked hell out of the son of a bitch, and I'll do it again. I wanted to let him know... I'm a white man and he's a damn nigger."

Zinn then crossed the street to Chief Pritchett's office. Pritchett was the gentler half of the good cop/bad cop relationship with Campbell. Campbell was quick to swing the club; Pritchett was more moderate, calling for medical aid to clean up the messes. It was institutionalized racism in its most violent, ugly extreme. For example, when King's six-month pregnant sister-in-law went to the jail with her three children to take food to a prisoner, a deputy sheriff beat her unconscious and caused her to miscarry.

Zinn asked Pritchett why he didn't arrest Campbell for assault. Pritchett just smiled. They parted with a handshake and Pritchett's next appointment walked in. It was Martin Luther King, Jr. King and Zinn

46

greeted each other. They were already acquainted from both being involved in the civil rights movement in Atlanta, Martin Luther King, Jr.'s birthplace.

Zinn's report about Albany to the Southern Regional Council became a front-page story in the *New York Times*. *The Nation* also published an article by Zinn about events in Albany called "Kennedy, the Reluctant Emancipator." Both articles stoked controversy and rage. When reporters asked Martin Luther King, Jr. if he agreed with the article in *The Nation*, he said he did, and pointed to the institutionalized racism of the FBI. This infuriated J. Edgar Hoover, the tyrannical head of the agency, who did not take criticism kindly. Zinn had actually aimed his criticisms not just at the FBI, but beyond it to the Department of Justice and

the White House itself. But the press only focused on the criticism of the FBI, and in Hoover's fury, he increasingly targeted King with wiretaps, surveillance, and harassment.

Zinn and Martin Luther King, Jr.

In 2002 Zinn told interviewer David Barsamian about his personal acquaintance with Marin Luther King, Jr. Zinn said that because he and King were both involved in Atlanta's close-knit black community, it was inevitable that they would meet during various social occasions. Zinn said that in person King was very different from the way he appeared when delivering one of his great orations. King was, "very low key," Zinn said, explaining that he was not the type to break into oratory or deliver stirring prose in everyday conversation. He was "very quiet," Zinn said, and "modest, thoughtful, measured, nothing of the charismatic leader showing in personal encounters."

On the other hand, according to Zinn, King's belief in nonviolence is often misunderstood or misconstrued. Because King was murdered, he is remembered as a martyr, but his being a martyr was incidental to his work, not the essence of it. He was not a martyr, in the sense of "one who willingly endures suffering for a cause." He was a man of action, who was courageous enough to take risks and sometimes endured suffering as a result of his activities.

NONVIOLENCE IS AN ACTION VERB!

When King was questioned about his belief in nonviolence, he would say that he did not want to take an absolutist point of view on the subject. People would ask, "What if your wife was being attacked?" And King would say, "I don't know what I would do in that situation, but I can tell you how I feel about the specific situation we are dealing with today." Though King sometimes went to jail in the course of taking action, he accepted it in the course of taking action, not because he believed it was a just response for him to be imprisoned for what he did.

Though King has been comfortably repackaged by today's media as a nice, mild-mannered man who claimed to "have a dream," in reality he was not passive, Zinn noted, and neither was Ghandi. The term the people in the southern movement used was not simply *nonviolence,* but *nonviolent direct action.* It was not passive; it was in fact very active, even aggressive, but nonviolent. The idea, Zinn said, was that if you're going to make progress against the established forces of repression, you must take action against it, but you do it nonviolently. Violence is something the establishment understands well and knows how to counter. Nonviolence, on the other hand, inhibits the use of violent retaliation by the establishment if there are observers to tell the story to the world.

Take a Look Around to Selma, Alabama

In 1963 Zinn's work with SNCC took him to Selma, the county seat of Dallas County, Alabama. Selma had been a slave market before the Civil War. In the post-slavery days, lynchings were common. In 1963, blacks were a substantial majority, 57 percent, of Selma's population, but the white minority kept a tight grip on power primarily by preventing blacks from voting. When Zinn arrived in Selma, only 1 percent of its blacks were registered to vote. If a black person tried to register, he or she would a number of impediments placed by the local government. To register to vote, one first had to apply, fill out a lengthy questionnaire, and take an oral examination. Blacks and whites were asked different questions. The information blacks were expected to provide was unrealistically difficult and insulting. For example, one such request was, "Summarize the Constitution of the United States."

When Zinn arrived in Selma in October 1963, the struggle for African Americans' right to vote was raging. Thirty-two black school teachers were fired for trying to register to vote. SNCC's John Lewis had been arrested for leading a picket line. Many others, including other SNCC members, had been arrested, and still more were brutally beaten or clubbed. The conflict led to war in the streets. If a black person wanted to exercise the right to vote, the old white establishment of Selma made it clear that that person risked life, limb, and skull for the audacity of making the attempt.

SNCC declared October 7 to be Freedom Day; and on that day they would try to register hundreds of people to vote. Dick Gregory, the comedian and writer, spoke boldly in the face of white segregationists at a church meeting, angry that his wife Lillian had been arrested in Selma while demonstrating. James Baldwin, the novelist, made a strong and eloquent stand. Selma was no longer an isolated microcosm where white supremacists could get away with murder and brutality. The world was watching. The twentieth century world of global media was descending on nineteenth century Jim Crow Alabama. The bold defiance of some civil rights advocates made Selma an international symbol of the struggle against oppression. As the old order approached its collision with the new breed of activists, the mounting tension was palpable.

Zinn was on the scene, taking notes minute by minute like a reporter as Freedom Day unfolded. At 9:30 a.m. the line at the Dallas County Courthouse began to form and grew until there were hundreds waiting to register to vote. Standing watch over them were helmeted members of the sheriff's posse, armed with guns and clubs. Four FBI agents and two Justice Department lawyers were also watching events unfold. It was their job to enforce the federal laws that protected the right of all Americans to vote. But so far the federal government had shown little interest in confronting the old order. Actions like Freedom Day were designed in part to bring world attention to the federal government's refusal to enforce the law against segregation and threaten government officials into taking action.

The sheriff and three armed deputies crossed the street to where two SNCC demonstrators were standing on the steps to

the federal building holding a sign that said "Register to Vote."
Within full view of the federal agents, the sheriff arrested them
for unlawful assembly.

There was no visible progress in the registration line. Zinn cal-
culated that the line moved so slowly that it would take many
years just to register the people who wanted to be registered.
Around noon the court announced that it would break for lunch.
At that point, no one could find a single black person who had
completed the registration process. People had been standing in
line for hours and were getting hungry and thirsty.

The sheriff was reinforced by a caravan of state police vehicles
that unloaded forty troopers with helmets, guns and clubs. There
were still only four federal officials on the scene. Jim Forman,
the executive director of SNCC, had telegraphed the Justice Department the night before, warning that there may be trouble at
the voter registration efforts, but had gotten no reply. Now with
the registration process stopped and people in line getting hungry, Forman and a local woman named Amelia Boynton approached the sheriff and said they wanted to get some food and
water to the people in line. The sheriff responded that the people would "not be molested in any way" and anyone attempting
to give them food would be arrested. Forman and Boynton
briefed reporters on what was happening and approached the
Justice Department officials hoping to get some support from
them in getting food to the people in line.

At 2 p.m. Zinn approached the senior federal attorney and asked
if there was any legitimate reason why the attorney couldn't
speak to the sheriff about allowing the people in line to get some
food. The attorney admitted that there was no legitimate reason
why the people in line should not be allowed to receive food, but
said he was not going to ask the question because he knew the
Justice Department and the Kennedy administration in Washington would not stand behind him.

Two SNCC workers were waiting with a shopping cart of food,
stymied now by the police and forbidden from giving anything to
the people in line. They decided to defy the police order. Zinn

and a group of photographers, newsmen, observers, and supporters approached the court house with the SNCC workers.

A trooper shouted out the order to move on. But the food carriers kept moving toward the people in line. A crowd of troopers jumped them, crowding tightly around them to

block the view of photographers, poking them with cattle prods, then manhandled them into their paddy wagon. Then they turned on the group that had accompanied the bearers of food and started pushing them around, trying to keep them from taking photographs. One of the police officers smashed the camera of a reporter with a club. A group of troopers threw the reporter up against a car, ripped his shirt, and backhanded him across the mouth.

Zinn and James Baldwin went into the FBI office and asked why they had not arrested the officers, who were obviously out of line. As a teacher of constitutional law, Zinn knew the law that said that any-one who uses any law to deprive someone of their civil rights would be subject to fine or imprisonment. The FBI man said he had no power to arrest the men under those circum-stances. But Zinn also re-cited the statute that said that FBI men had the au-thority to make arrests without warrants when laws were violated.

That night organizers held a meeting in a church to celebrate the day's activities. In fact, little had changed. The walls of resistance against racial equality had not come tumbling down. The proportion of black voters in Selma who were registered to vote, was still only 1 percent. But it was unprecedented that 350 people had stood in line and defied ob-stacles and intimidation to assert their right to vote. It was one small step and it would take many more like it to achieve any real progress. But it was still cause for celebration. As history now shows, the walls protecting segregation did eventually fall. And, it took many such relatively small, individual actions to bring about that major change.

Zinn wrote an article for the New Republic narrating the events of the day. It embarrassed and angered the Justice Department. The chief of its civil rights division wrote an indignant letter to the New Republic saying the proper place for the civil rights struggle was in the courts and that the Justice Department had two cases pending in Selma. He ignored the fact that the FBI could have acted that day.

In 1965 Zinn returned to Selma. By then it had attracted international attention when local authorities brought the hammer down on anti-segregation demonstrations, with mass arrests, the murder by clubbing of a white minister, the shooting of a black man, and many bloody beatings. President Lyndon Johnson federalized the Alabama National Guard to watch over a planned fifty-four-mile march for civil rights from Selma to Montgomery, Alabama.

Zinn took on a writing assignment for *The Nation* for which he would visit the South and take stock of the changes one hundred years after the Civil War ended. His tour took him to Lynchburg, Virginia; John's Island, South Carolina; Vicksburg, Mississippi; and then to Selma to join the march to Montgomery. Three hundred people started the march and their ranks increased as it progressed. This particular event occurred without casualties, with the protection of the military. Things were slowly changing. The work, struggles, bloodshed, and deaths were not for nothing.

The Birth of a Writing Career

While Zinn was chair of the Department of History at Spelman from 1956 to 1963, he also carried on academic pursuits beyond the school. He received his PhD from Columbia in 1958, was a postdoctoral fellow in East Asian Studies at Harvard University in 1960 and 1961, and was the director of Non-Western Studies at Atlanta University in 1961 and 1962. In addition to teaching and writing his dissertation, Zinn spent the summers in 1957 and 1958 in Denver, Colorado, studying the use of documentary film in teaching history.

It was during Zinn's years at Spelman that he began his writing career and eventually became a prolific writer of many published articles, essays, and books. The subject of his doctoral dissertation was the congressional career of Fiorello LaGuardia, who had been the three term mayor of New York from 1934 to 1945. "Conscience of the Jazz Age: LaGuardia in Congress" won a prize from American Historical Association, which sponsored its publication by Cornell University Press as *LaGuardia in Congress* in 1959. It was to be Zinn's first book of many.

His first published article was in Harpers magazine in 1959. It was called "A Fate Worse than Integration," and it became basis for his larger essay, "The Southern Mystique," published in *The American Scholar.* (For more on writing pursuits, see the section titled "Zinn's Writing.")

Greenwood, Mississippi

Howard and Roslyn Zinn went to Mississippi in 1963 to work with SNCC, but as Zinn said, "work" is a very neutral sounding word for what was happening there. It was during this period that Zinn began to contemplate the ideas that would define his contribution to the reporting of history, including the observation that most history books leave out the struggles of the majority of ordinary people who truly create history, and instead only focus on a few major symbolic people and events that portray a general arc of history.

The resistance against recognizing black people as equal citizens was deadly in the South and it took the deaths and brutalizing of many people before that resistance could be worn down. Merely to try to register black people to vote in Mississippi in the early '60s was to take your life into your hands. Like in Selma, the segregationists were determined to make sure blacks did not achieve any political power.

Zinn became friends with Bob Moses, a young light-skinned African American man from Harlem who had moved down to Mississippi to work with local blacks, helping them to realize their rights and register to vote. For his efforts he had been knifed, beaten, thrown in jail, and threatened with murder. Not long after he had arrived in Mississippi, Moses told Zinn that he had been asked to examine the body of a black man, the father of nine children who had been killed by a white man with whom he had been arguing. The white man just walked up and shot him in the head. He was acquitted because of a black witness, who said it had been self defense. Later the witness recanted his story and told the truth—that it was cold-blooded murder. After recanting he was killed in his front yard by three shotgun blasts. The killings ignited protests in the black community. Over one hundred high school students stayed out of school. Many who protested were beaten or jailed.

Zinn also got to know Sam Block, a young son of a construction worker from a small town in Mississippi who was also trying to help local black people gain rights. As he went from door to door asking people what their needs were, he was shadowed by a police car, making people afraid to open their doors. One day, three white men jumped him and beat him up. Another time a truck tried to run him over and he barely escaped by getting behind a telephone pole.

Block took up the cause of a fourteen-year-old boy who had been charged with burglary though he claimed to be at work picking cotton when the crime was committed. Police stripped him, threw him on a concrete floor, bullwhipped him, and beat him with fists, a club, and a blackjack. Block photographed the boy's wounds, took an affidavit from him telling his side of the story, and sent them to the Justice Department in Washington. This angered the police and intensified the street war. But it also inspired local blacks to take a stand and join the cause. More of them started attending the SNCC meetings and more tried to register to vote. The assault on them continued. One night Block and two other SNCC members were working late when a gang barged into the office with guns and chains. The SNCC members escaped out the window and onto the roof next door.

There were shotgun blasts in people's homes and cars, attack dogs turned on protestors, and an onslaught of deadly intimidation, but it did not stop the people from demanding their rights. The more blacks resisted, the more people were inspired to join the movement.

The summer of 1964 was designated Freedom Summer in Mississippi by SNCC, along with the National Association for the Advancement of Colored People (NAACP), the Congress of Racial Equality (CORE), and the Southern Christian Leadership Conference (SCLC). Howard and Roz Zinn spent the summer there; Roz worked in SNCC's Jackson office and Howard taught in the Freedom Schools, where black children were educated in the democratic process.

Howard believed that Mississippi would never be the same again after the Freedom Summer. It would be years before segregation ended, and even then racism would not be eradicated. But there was a marked change in the South. It was clear that progress was taking place and the old system of segregation was breaking down while a new world was born. Years later, when Zinn reunited with people he shared those struggles with, they would reminisce about the horrors of the times, and agreed that, despite the struggles, they were the best years of their lives.

On to Boston

During the months after being fired from Spelman, Zinn was very active in the civil rights struggle. He also wrote two books on the civil rights movement during that year, and edited a volume called *New Deal Thought*. In the book, Zinn examined the New Deal and claimed it was a step in the right direction, but ultimately found it insufficient. (See "Zinn's Writing" for more on this work.)

During his search for a new job, he called Boston University, where he had previously lectured on the conditions in the South. He was invited to join the political science department. In his first year, he taught a course in the fall semester called "Civil Liberties" and a course in the spring semester called "Introduction to Political Theory." His courses were packed with two to four hundred students each.

He found textbooks dull, so he went beyond them and referred his students to classic literature. His favorites included Arthur Miller's *The Crucible*, Ron Kovic's *Born on the Fourth of July*, Richard Wright's *Black Boy*, and Dalton Trumbo's *Johnny Got His Gun*. His teaching style was improvisational. He would come to class with stacks of paper full of notes and quotations, and would begin his lecture by drawing on his material in a free-form manner. He was unconcerned with grades. He assumed that those who wanted to learn would, and those who didn't want to wouldn't. He quickly became one of Boston University's most popular teachers.

War and Resistance

The mid-sixties were tumultuous years, years of social upheaval, the dying of one world and the birth of another. The year 1963, when Zinn was fired from Spelman, was the same year that President John F. Kennedy was assassinated, setting the tone for what would become a very violent decade. Between 1961 and 1963, Kennedy had escalated the U.S. involvement from six hundred military advisers to sixteen thousand. But he was wavering and had issued an executive order to begin bringing advisers back. When Kennedy was ambushed in Dallas on November 22, 1963, he was replaced by Lyndon Johnson, who immediately reversed Kennedy's order to withdraw one thousand military advisers from Vietnam, and instead Johnson sent the first combat troops. It was the beginning of a huge escalation of the war that was to drag on into the 1970s, creating deep rifts within the social fabric of the nation.

The battles against segregation, on the other hand, had made progress. In 1964, when Zinn started teaching at Boston University, President Johnson pushed the civil rights legislation that Kennedy had introduced in Congress. The bill reaffirmed rights that had already been guaranteed in the Constitution, but which were denied in practice to African Americans. The legislation was designed to give "all Americans the right to be served in facilities which are open to the public—hotels, restaurants, theaters, retail stores, and similar establishments," as well as "greater protection for the right to vote."

The Civil Rights Act of 1964 expanded on the Civil Rights Act of 1957, which had been primarily a voting rights bill. It expanded and made more explicit the government's mandate to support Constitutional rights for all people. It was a milestone that made civil rights the law of the land, gave a new level of recognition to civil rights for all people, and reduced the urgency of racial issues. Meanwhile, the war in Vietnam was churning up and rapidly taking center stage as the most urgent civil rights issue of all. Being refused the right to sit at a lunch counter was one thing, but being forced to kill and die for reasons no one seemed to be able to credibly explain was a great deal worse.

The same year that the Civil Rights bill was passed, Johnson used a trumped up incident in Vietnam's Gulf of Tonkin as a pretext for drastically escalating the war in Vietnam. The government's story was that an American destroyer on a "routine patrol" was attacked. In fact, there was no evidence that there really was an attack, and secondly, it was not a routine patrol—it was a spying mission in foreign waters thousands of miles from the U.S. President Johnson used the incident to get Congress to give him wide latitude to step up his attacks on Vietnam.

JINGO, JINGO ALL THE WAY.

At that time, Zinn had no way of knowing if the claim of the incident at Tonkin was true, but he did know some relevant history. The U.S. had given military aid to the French in its attempt to hold Vietnam as a colony, and when France finally gave up, the U.S. stepped in and took over. Vietnam was rich in resources that interested American industrialists, including coal, iron ore, tin, copper, lead, zinc, nickel, manganese, titanium, chromite, tungsten, bauxite, apatite, graphite, mica, silica sand, and limestone.

The American government took the position that Vietnam might fall under the influence of Communists, and if so it would lead to a chain reaction of countries falling like dominoes stacked in a line to the Communists. The U.S. government propped up the dictatorial regime in Saigon and portrayed the war as a battle between two countries: North Vietnam, a Communist country, and South Vietnam, a democratic country. The South Vietnamese government was not democratic, but served the interests of the Americans, in return for American military and financial support. The puppet government rejected elections under U.S. orders and violently suppressed all resistance.

Zinn also knew the history of American expansionism. The U.S. had expanded by killing or forcing out indigenous people who had lived in the country for thousands of years; in a short time, the American government had built up an empire, taking over Spain's Florida colonies by attacking Mexico and claiming half its land before using military power to establish U.S. control in Cuba, Puerto Rico, Haiti, the Dominican Republic, Hawaii, the Philippines, and Central America. So he was skeptical of the government's pronouncements about its supposedly noble efforts to protect freedom and democracy by attacking Vietnam.

He knew it was common for a government to use phony incidents as pretexts for wars. President Polk had used a skirmish between Mexican and American troops as justification for starting the Mexican War. The fight had broken out on disputed territory, but that didn't stop Polk from proclaiming that "American blood has been shed on American soil" as a rallying war cry. Polk's own diaries revealed that he was looking for an excuse to take Mexican territory and the incident provided it.

The U.S. blamed the bombing of the battleship *Maine* in Cuba on the Spanish and used it as an excuse to go to war against Spain, but the government's claims were never proven. The incident did, however, justify pushing the Spanish out of Cuba and installing a U.S. presence there. The U.S. government found another set of convenient circumstances to seize the Philippines. The sinking of the *Lusitania,* which was the justification for the U.S. entry into World War I was another trumped up incident. While the government claimed a passenger ship had been sunk by ruthless German submarines, the *Lusitania* was actually carrying munitions, participating in the war undercover with its papers altered to make it appear to be a passenger ship.

In the Vietnam War, the U.S. government claimed to be defending the right of the Vietnamese people for self-determination, the right to choose their own government. But Zinn knew that the U.S. government had fought against self-determination in other countries, like Iran, where the CIA engineered a coup in 1954 to restore the Shah to power to protect the interests of oil companies, and in Guatemala, where the U.S. invaded in 1954 to

WELCOME HOME, SHAH.

protect the interests of the United Fruit Company. The U.S. in fact supported vicious dictators all over the world, as long as they served the interests of U.S. corporations: Batista in Cuba, Somoza in Nicaragua, Suharto in Indonesia, Trujillo in the Dominican Republic, and Marcos in the Philippines to name a few.

Now the U.S. government was bombing civilians in Vietnam, and Zinn felt sure it was not justified by the political claims. Zinn's civil rights allies were increasingly turning against the war, people like Bob Moses, who objected to Johnson's willingness to send troops around the world for some cause no one could understand, not authorizing troops to protect the rights of citizens to vote in America.

A disproportionate number of soldiers being sent to Vietnam were black and the war was becoming the most urgent civil rights issue in America. It violated the civil rights of a broad spectrum of people, including Americans of all ethnicities and the Vietnamese people. The government's act of sending thousands, and eventually millions, of young Americans against their will to fight in Southeast Asia became the most pressing issue for young Americans. Rebellions broke out on college campuses across the country. The issue of the Vietnam War united the youth of all races against a single issue, a single form of oppression.

The U.S. still had a military draft in place from World War II and as the Vietnam War escalated, and the Johnson administration's objectives continued to fail, draft calls went up, and more and more Americans found themselves ordered to go to Vietnam. The American death toll reached 58,000, the number of wounded American soldiers was near 304,000, and there were millions of Vietnamese casualties. The war reached into the homes of Americans; college students, who were of draft age, protested the war in greater and greater numbers. Zinn turned his attentions, along with many other activists, from civil rights to the struggle against the war. The civil rights struggle merged with the resistance to an unjust war.

Zinn plunged in, proud to become part of a tradition of Americans resisting the threat of imprisonment for a cause they could not believe in. War resistance had a history in America going back to the colonists who resisted conscription into British wars against the French. Zinn shared and supported the convictions of the majority of young people who faced the draft, who believed that the war was not worth dying for, and was an immoral, unjustified attack on another country with which the American people had no real quarrel. His anti-war beliefs began to express themselves in his writing and activities. Beginning in early 1966, Zinn published a number of articles regarding the conflict in Vietnam:

"Vietnam: Means and Ends," "Negroes and Vietnam," and "Vietnam: The Logic of Withdrawal," which he later developed into a book by the same name that sold through eight printings. Zinn later named *Vietnam: The Logic of Withdrawal* as his second favorite of all the books in his whole career, after *A People's History of the United States*. That year the number of U.S. soldiers in Vietnam reached half a million.

By 1967 attendance at anti-war rallies had grown into the thousands. In October 1967, Zinn spoke at a rally that five thousand people attended, where over two hundred people burned their draft cards. It was one of many such demonstrations taking place throughout the country. The next day thousands gathered for a rally at the Lincoln Memorial in Washington and marched to the Pentagon, where they were met by thousands of soldiers.

While Zinn taught at Boston University, there were many rallies, occupations of buildings, and teach-ins that lasted through the night. In one incident, a thousand students stood shoulder-to-shoulder for five days in a chapel with a deserting soldier, supporting his right for sanctuary, until federal agents finally forced their way through the crowd and seized the soldier.

Trip to Vietnam

In January 1968 Zinn got a phone call from David Dellinger, a peace activist he had met in Hiroshima the year before. Dellinger said he had received a telegram from the North Vietnamese government offering to release three captive American pilots as a gesture of peace. The North Vietnamese wanted the peace movement to designate a representative to go to Hanoi to meet the pilots upon their release. Leaders of the peace movement had chosen Zinn and Father Daniel Berrigan, a Catholic priest, antiwar activist and poet, to make the trip. The next day Zinn went to New York City and met Berrigan, Dellinger, and Tom Hayden, another antiwar leader. During their meeting, a State Department representative came to the door. He claimed that the government learned about the arrangement and wanted to endorse the trip, to stamp their passports. Without the approval of the government,

it was illegal to travel to North Vietnam and other Communist countries. But Berrigan and Zinn declined to take the government's endorsement.

The air trip took twenty eight hours, with stops in Copenhagen, Frankfurt, Teheran, Calcutta, and Bangkok. At every stop a State Department representative would get on the plane and offer to stamp their passports. They declined each offer. They arrived in Vientiane, Laos, but going farther was not possible because of the Tet offensive, when the Viet Cong burst out of apparent retreat and launched a series of surprise attacks all over South Vietnam, even occupying the U.S. embassy. After a brief time in Laos, Zinn and Berrigan were taken to Hanoi, but during their first night they were awakened by sirens signaling an air raid. It was the first time the former bombardier had been on the receiving end of a bombing raid.

THIS IRONY I COULD LIVE WITHOUT.

After five days of air raids, they were finally introduced to the prisoners they had come to meet. They met the three pilots, and the next day there was a ceremony for their release. The pilots were the first prisoners of war to be released by the Vietnamese since the U.S. had begun bombing.

Zinn and Berrigan became friends during their three weeks together on the trip. Later Berrigan participated in a protest in which he broke into a draft board and poured napalm on draft records. He and the other participants were sentenced to three years in prison. During the appeal process Berrigan disappeared and remained a fugitive for four months with Zinn's assistance on some occasions.

The Fall of Johnson, the Rise of Nixon

In 1968 anti-war sentiment was so powerful that Johnson had to cancel all appearances except at military bases. Then after Eugene McCarthy, a practically unknown Democrat running on an anti-war platform, won 40 percent of the vote in the first Democratic primary, Johnson announced he would not seek re-election.

Robert F. Kennedy threw his hat into the race on an anti-war platform and soon moved to the head of Democratic contenders, but was assassinated in Los Angeles on the day he won the California primary. In the 1968 Democratic convention, the party nominated Hubert Humphrey, who had been Johnson's vice president and would not repudiate the actions of the Johnson administration. To anti-war activists Humphrey's nomination was a denial of the anti-war fervor that had driven Johnson from office. Even though Kennedy had moved into first place on an anti-war platform, the party bosses had gone into the proverbial backroom and emerged with a candidate who represented the repudiated war policies. Thousands demonstrated in the streets of Chicago and the Chicago police responded with extreme force, beating and jailing many in what an official report later called a "police riot."

With the extreme rage against the war at that point, both candidates promised they would end the war. In the closing days of the campaign, Nixon claimed to have "a secret plan" to end it, though it was never revealed or referred to once he became president in 1969. Once he took office, he increased the violence in Vietnam, expanding the war with bombings in the North, as if his secret plan had really been to beat the Vietnamese into submission. But violence had not succeeded in bringing the Vietnamese to surrender in the past and increasing it did not work for Nixon. Meanwhile, he feared the country was becoming ungovernable and grew increasingly desperate.

The Pentagon Papers

In the early 1970s Zinn found himself once again at the center of the cyclone of radical American politics. It began in the late 1960s when Daniel Ellsberg, a former consultant to the RAND Corporation, got hold of a document from the Pentagon called *United States–Vietnam Relations, 1945–1967: A Study Prepared by the Department of Defense*. It was a 47-volume, 7,000-page, top-secret Department of Defense history of the United States' involvement in Vietnam, from the beginning and told by the perpetrators of the war. Ellsberg sent a copy of the document to Howard and Roslyn Zinn, who then enlisted the help of Noam Chomsky to form a team to edit and annotate the document for publication. The document was published as "The Pentagon Papers" in the *New York Times* beginning June 13, 1971. The Pentagon Papers created a huge controversy because they revealed that the government purposely misled the American people about what it was doing in Vietnam. While President Johnson was telling the American people that he would not expand the war, he was in fact doing just that with air strikes in Laos and coastal raids of North Vietnam.

The publication of the documents embarrassed and angered the top officials of the U.S. government. Assistant Attorney General William Rehnquist (later promoted to Chief Justice by Nixon) tried to stop the documents from being published through injunctions. To Nixon, it was a case of spying, treason, the stealing of state secrets—a replay of the case of Julius and Ethel Rosenberg, who were executed in 1953 for giving nuclear secrets to the Soviets. According to Nixon's reasoning, Ellsberg was a traitor who should be put to death. Howard and Roslyn Zinn and Chomsky would have been his accomplices, according to that reasoning, and so would the *New York Times.* But rather than giving military secrets to an enemy country during war, the Pentagon Papers were released to the American people, those who were being lied to, improperly, according to Ellsberg, Zinn, and Chomsky. The case went to the Supreme Court and was so controversial that each of the nine justices wrote a separate opinion.

The publication of the Pentagon Papers so enraged Nixon that he lost all sense of proportion in his quest for revenge. He wanted to make an example out of Ellsberg, to destroy him and intimidate all would-be whistle blowers. He arranged for some of his hirelings break into the office of Ellsberg's psychiatrist in search of information he could use to smear Ellsberg. Nixon's burglars, led by ex-CIA agent E. Howard Hunt, were called "the Plumbers;" it was their job to stop leaks. The Plumbers got away with that break in, but they were not so lucky when they went on to break into the Democratic Party headquarters in the Watergate Hotel in Washington, D.C. As the investigation of the crime closed in on Richard Nixon, it set up a series of events that forced Nixon, who had won by a large majority, to step down from office. The publishing of Pentagon Papers turned out to be a significant factor in Nixon's resignation.

Ellsberg was charged with theft, conspiracy, and espionage for taking the document. Zinn was called as an expert witness by the defense. He discussed the history of Vietnam for several hours on the stand. He explained that the information in the Pentagon Papers could not be used to harm the United States. Rather, its significance was to show how the government had systematically lied to the American people, arguably a crime itself, or at least an abuse of power. A federal judge dismissed the case, saying it had been tainted by Nixon's burglary of Ellsberg's psychiatrist's office.

End of the Vietnam War

In early 1973, after four years of negotiation in Paris, the U.S. government signed a treaty with the government of North Vietnam agreeing to withdraw. The war continued between the government of Hanoi in the North and what remained of the colonial government of Saigon, with the U.S. continuing to give military aid to Saigon. Finally in early 1975, the government of South Vietnam collapsed and the war was over. Vietnam was united as a single republic.

A People's History

In 1980 Zinn published *A People's History of the United States,* a book that changed his life, become his most important work and changed the way history was conceptualized for millions of people. Zinn says that the book took twenty years from conception of its fundamental ideas to publication. The actual writing took less than a year to complete. He wrote *People's History,* he said, because the political activist movements of the 1960s had led to an evolution in consciousness, a transformation of how people saw the world, and the old histories were not adequate to speak to that new frame of mind. People wanted histories that showed how working people, Indians, slaves and women lived. None of the existing histories did that, so he set out to provide the book himself.

"I wanted to tell the story of American history from the standpoint of women, Black people, Indians, of working people and of radicals and protesters," he told *Revolutionary*

Worker in 1998. "As soon as I made that decision, it was clear this was going to be a different kind of history. And I have no doubt that the reason my book has reached so many people—to my surprise, actually, and certainly to the surprise of the publisher—is that people who read it were suddenly struck by the fact that I was telling American history from a very different viewpoint." The book has sold about 100,000 copies per year since publication, nearly two million copies as of this writing.

Beyond the University

During Zinn's tenure at Boston University, he worked as a visiting professor at the University of Paris during the years 1974, 1978, and 1984. In 1988, after twenty-four years as a political science teacher at Boston University, Zinn retired from the university to devote himself full time to writing, speaking, activism, and other

A LOTTA GOODWILL IN HERE.

PEOPLE'S HISTORY OF THE UNITED STATES

related projects. He became more prolific than ever before.

Zinn in the Movies

In 1997 the Academy Award-winning film *Good Will Hunting*, written by Matt Damon and Ben Affleck and starring Damon, Affleck, and Robin Williams, Will Hunting tells his teacher that the book *People's History of the United States* "will knock you on your ass." Damon, in fact, knew Zinn since he was five years old. They were next door neighbors in South Boston.

Years later Zinn and Damon became partners, along with Ben Affleck and Chris Moore, as executive producers of a project to make a miniseries out of *People's History of the United States*. The idea was to film certain sequences from the book. Though the project has been discussed with News Corporation (the parent company of Fox) and HBO, both have dropped negotiations and the film has yet to be produced.

Zinn on Iraq

In keeping with his anti-war stance, Zinn opposed the invasion and occupation of Iraq by the Bush administration in 2003. But his opposition was not just to the occupation of Iraq. He saw the matter as much more serious. In *The Guardian* in August 2005, he wrote, "More ominous, perhaps, than the occupation of Iraq is the occupation of the U.S. I wake up in the morning, read the newspaper, and feel that we are an occupied country, that some alien group has taken over. I wake up thinking: the U.S. is in the grip of a president surrounded by thugs in suits who care nothing about human life abroad or here, who care nothing about freedom abroad or here, who care nothing about what happens to the earth, the water, or the air, or what kind of world will be inherited by our children and grandchildren."

Calling for Truth about 9/11

In 2004, Zinn signed a document called "9/11 Truth Statement," which said:

We Want Real Answers about 9/11. On August 31, 2004, Zogby International, the official North American political polling agency for Reuters, released a poll that found nearly half (49.3%) of New York City residents and 41% of those in New York state believe U.S. leaders had foreknowledge of impending 9/11 attacks and "consciously failed" to act. Of the New York City residents, 66% called for a new probe of unanswered questions by Congress or the New York Attorney General. In connection with this news, we have assembled 100 notable Americans and 40 family members of those who died to sign this 9/11 Statement, which calls for immediate public attention to unanswered questions that suggest that people within the current administration may indeed have deliberately allowed 9/11 to happen, perhaps as a pretext for war.

The statement went on to ask twelve specific questions about the incident, including the following:

Why were standard operating procedures for dealing with hijacked airliners not followed that day? Why were the extensive missile batteries and air defenses reportedly deployed around the Pentagon not activated during the attack? Why did the Secret Service allow Bush to complete his elementary school visit, apparently unconcerned about his safety or that of the schoolchildren? Why hasn't a single person been fired, penalized, or reprimanded for the gross incompetence we witnessed that day? Why haven't authorities in the U.S. and abroad published the results of multiple investigations into trading that strongly suggested foreknowledge of specific details of the 9/11 attacks, resulting in tens of millions of dollars of traceable gains? How could Flight 77, which reportedly hit the Pentagon, have flown back toward Washington, D.C. for 40 minutes without being detected by the FAA's radar or the even superior radar possessed by the US military?

In this matter there is a divergence between Zinn the historian and seeker of justice and Zinn the activist. He does not believe the government's story on the subject, but as an activist he is a pragmatist and is wary of expending much time trying to figure out what happened that day. In 2008, he told this author that "it's one of those controversies that leads nowhere, is a diversion from what needs to be done. Whatever happened on 9/11, and that is not clear, what is clear is that the Bush Administration used 9/11 as an excuse to go to war and throw the country into fear and take absolute power in the government and destroy the Constitution. That is what we should be concentrating our energy on, and not engaging in a fruitless, endless argument about what really happened on 9/11."

Zinn on Bush

In October 2004, an interviewer for *Guernica* magazine asked Zinn how important he thought the 2004 election was between Kerry and Bush, and he said, "It's very important—because we are in the thrall of a very dangerous regime, more dangerous than any presidency I can remember. Kind of a runaway group of people who seem not to care about the opinions of the rest of the world, not to care either about the majority of Americans who now oppose the war. They have their own agenda and they are trying to take total power. I mean, here's a president who gets 47 or 48 percent of the vote—loses the popular vote, in fact, to his opponent—and takes 100 percent of the power as soon as he takes office, as if he had a mandate. He didn't have a mandate from the American people. He snuck into the presidency with the aid of political cronies, his father's having appointed members of the Supreme Court, his brother governor of Florida. And then he takes total control."

Zinn told Robert Birnbaum (at identitytheory.com) in 2001, "Here the guy wins the presidency by the most nefarious of methods and without a popular mandate. Losing a popular vote by a larger margin than Hayes lost the popular vote in 1876, but then moves ahead with aplomb, with total arrogance as if the country is his. My feeling is that we are living in an occupied country. Really, that we've been taken over, a junta has taken power and now the problem for the American people is to do what people do in an occupied country."

The Zinn Vision

In 1998 *Revolutionary Worker* interviewed Zinn and asked him what his vision would be for a different kind of world. He answered that it is "a vision of the world in which powerful corporations did not dominate the economy... in which economic enterprises were controlled by the people who worked in them... and in which the rights of workers and consumers were represented in the decision-making bodies. It would be a world in which we had a kind of grass-roots democracy that existed in the

Paris Commune in 1871... constant participation... meetings of people all over, where people's political participation wasn't confined to voting every two years or every four years, to choosing between two miserable possibilities... a kind of grass-roots participation and decision-making at every possible level. Those are not easy to achieve in very complicated, large-scale societies. But I think it is certainly possible to have infinitely more political democracy than we have today. And the object would be to really equalize the conditions of people in the world, to use the enormous wealth that exists in this world to feed people, to take care of their children. Everybody should be assured of fundamental things of life—everybody should be assured of a place to live, enough food, of care for their children, and everybody should be assured of health care without worrying about bills, or forms, or signatures. And we need a breaking down of national barriers—a world without passports and visas, where people are free to move in the way corporations are now free to move across national boundaries. Obviously this is a vision hard to contemplate. But I think that unless you have such a vision, you are not in a position to evaluate what is going on day to day."

Zinn's Hope for America's Future

In April 2008, during the primary season of the presidential election, Wajahat Ali interviewed Zinn for Counterpunch.org, and asked him if he had any hope for America's future. Zinn answered, "The present situation for the U.S. looks grim, but I am

hopeful, as I see the American people waking up and being overwhelmingly opposed to this war and to the Bush regime, as I reflect on movements in history and how they arose surprisingly when they seemed defeated. I believe the American people have the capacity to create a new movement, which would change the direction of our nation from being a military power to being a peaceful nation, using our enormous wealth for human needs, here and abroad."

Zinn on Obama, FDR, and Lincoln

Zinn has said that his favorite president is Franklin D. Roosevelt because he responded to the economic crisis of the 1930s and to the protests with a sensitivity that is rare among presidents. He also has written that FDR did not go far enough in his reform of the system. He has said that although Lincoln was a politician first, and did not come into office or conduct the war based on ending slavery, he did in the end become an important force in that cause. The abolitionist Wendell Phillips had been critical of Lincoln's cautiousness in regard to the abolition of slavery, but nevertheless saw great possibilities in Lincoln's election. Though Lincoln was not himself an abolitionist, Phillips said, he had the potential, if the people acted vigorously, to be transformed like a pawn on a chessboard that becomes a queen, to "sweep the board." He speaks of Obama in similar terms. Near the end of the campaign, Zinn endorsed Obama's candidacy.

"Obama, like Lincoln, tends to look first at his political fortunes instead of making his decisions on moral grounds," wrote Zinn at Commondreams.org after the 2008 election, "But, as the first African American in the White House, elected by an enthusiastic citizenry which expects a decisive move towards peace and social justice, he presents a possibility for important change."

Obama can reach his potential to be a great president, Zinn says, if he creates a radical turnaround from the militaristic foreign policy that has ruled during the Bush years, and too often in American history. If Obama can effect such a turnaround, show the world that the U.S. is a peace-seeking nation and negotiate with other world leaders to reduce military stockpiles, billions of dollars can be freed up to improve the lives of people. Obama should emulate FDR and give America a new New Deal, said Zinn.

Lone Traveler

Roslyn Zinn died May 14, 2008, of cancer. She was eighty-five. In her last twenty years, she retired from her work as a teacher and social worker to become a painter, producing many figurative paintings, landscapes and still lifes. After she found out

ROSLYN

she had cancer, she spent the summer doing a lot of swimming and said it was the best summer of her life. She and Howard were married sixty-four years. She was involved in editing all of his books and many of his articles.

In the introduction to "Painting Life," a collection of Roslyn Zinn's work that was published in 2007 she wrote: "After years as a teacher and social worker, I turned seriously to painting, which throughout my life had sparked and enlivened my spirit," Ms. Zinn wrote in a brief a few months after she was diagnosed with ovarian cancer. "What I see in the world, so burdened and troubled, and yet beautiful in nature and in the human form, impels me to seek to create images that give the possibility of hope."

Failure to Quit

Zinn continues to be active in politics, writing articles, giving interviews, and speaking at events. Now in his eighties he is still a vital voice for the causes he has stood for his entire life.

Asked where he got the courage to take stands throughout his life as both a historian and an activist, he told Harry Kreisler, "It's not a courage to me, it's a sad commentary, that we think it requires a lot of courage just to speak your mind. I'm not going to be executed. I'm not even going to be given a long jail sentence. I may be thrown into jail for a day or two, and that has happened to me eight to nine times. I may be fired, I may get a salary decrease, but these are pitiful things compared to what happens to people in the world. So it doesn't take much courage to do that. I had two friends, my closest friends in the Air Force, both of whom were killed in the last weeks of the war, and I think after you've been through a war experience, and after you've been aware of people dying, and somebody says, 'Are you willing to risk your job? Are you willing to risk a salary cut? Are you willing to risk that you won't get tenure?'—these are pitiful risks compared to the risks that people have taken in the world."

Asked in 2008 what strategy he envisions for restoring democratic power to a country then still under the control of the very anti-democratic Bush regime, he told this author, "There are no magic formulas, no startling new tactics. It's a matter of persisting and expanding whatever we have been doing—and truth is, it's working. More and more people see the futility of war, more and more people see that our economic system is both inefficient and unjust, and we have to keep eroding the supports for the system until it crumbles. It takes persistence and patience and confidence that if we just continue small and seemingly meaningless and undramatic efforts, change will come."

Zinn: The Work

A People's History of the United States

A People's History of the United States, published in 1980, is Zinn's magnum opus, his major, essential work. It provides the perspective through which his career and his legacy can best be understood. In a sense, to know *People's History* is to know Zinn. In this 650-page volume, written during less than a year of intense productivity, Zinn laid out a new paradigm that was to re-define history, and to create a new model for what would become a new alternative history. It is not only Zinn's principle work; it is one of the most influential books on history and politics of its time. It therefore deserves special attention in any discussion of Zinn and his work.

As its name implies, it is a history from the point of view of the working people, the people of the class Zinn himself was a member of, not from the point of view of the rulers, conquerors and masters from whose point of view history is traditionally presented. This is the story of America from point of view of the vast majority, those who have the least to gain from the exploits and adventures of the masters and inevitably bear the brunt of them.

People's History focuses specifically on the struggles of working people in a rapidly expanding capitalist industrial system. It maintains a tight focus on its theme, which is what enables the book to plow through five hundred years of history in only 650 pages and still create a vivid story. At the same time, it leaves out vast areas of the history, including many events that are extremely well known. Zinn recognizes no need to be comprehensive in his single volume history of a very large, broad story. He remains narrowly concentrated on the story he wants to tell of the struggles of working people, a story largely ignored before.

People's History is iconoclastic, knocking the traditional celebrated figures from their pinnacles and exposing all their human weaknesses, their greed, selfishness, brutality, hypocrisy, dishonesty, ambition, and cruelty. Zinn shows an unpalatable truth: History is not pretty. Some call the book revisionist history, and it may be seen as an altered vision of the past, leading to an altered vision of the present and of the possibilities of the future. *People's History* creates a basis for building a new, more realistic history.

The book is jarring to Americans because, as *New York Times* reviewer Eric Foner said, it is "a reshuffling of heroes and villains." A historian himself and professor of history at Columbia University, Foner said the book "bears the same relationship to traditional history as a photographic negative does to a print: The areas of darkness and light have been reversed." Foner, and other reviewers, praised Zinn's ability to choose quotations that vividly portrayed and dramatized the story. But Foner also criticized the book, saying that the approach was limited, that the groups it focuses on–blacks, Indians, women and laborers–"appear either as rebels or victims" and "less dramatic but more typical lives—people struggling to survive with dignity in difficult circumstances—receive little attention." Foner called the book, "a deeply pessimistic vision of the American experience," but at the same time said it should be "required reading for a new generation of students now facing conscription."

A review in the *Library Journal* called *People's History* "an excellent antidote to establishment history" that tells the story "from the point of view of those who have been exploited politically and economically and whose plight has been largely omitted from most histories."

The book has sold nearly two million copies, making it one of the most popular history books of all time. It has been updated a few times since its original publication in 1980 and its recent editions cover the period from Columbus's discovery of the New World through 9/11 and what George W. Bush called "The War on Terror" (which Zinn generously corrects to "War on Terrorism").

A People's History of the United States has spawned many offspring, many written by Zinn himself, and others written by other authors. Zinn wrote *A Young People's History of the United States,* as well as *A People's History of American Empire,* which is a graphic novel/comic book telling of the story. With David Williams, Zinn wrote *A People's History of the Civil War: Struggles for the Meaning of Freedom.* There is *The Twentieth Century: A People's History* and *Voices of a People's History of the United States,* which is a sort of documentary history, telling the story through first-hand accounts, journal entries, speeches, personal letters, and published opinion pieces. With Vijay Prashad he wrote *Darker Nations: A People's History of the Third World.* Other authors have taken up the theme with People's Histories of the world, the American Revolution, sports, the Supreme Court, science, and poverty. Following is a brief summary and discussion of Zinn's view of American history as it is presented in *A People's History.*

Columbus's Discovery of the New World

The book begins like a nuclear explosion obliterating the foundation of the standard view of traditional history textbooks, focusing first on Columbus's discovery of America, a new world for the European empires to plunder. Zinn's story of Columbus is stripped of the romantic trappings traditionally taught to schoolchildren. In textbooks Columbus is a courageous explorer who sailed beyond the point that most people thought was the end of the earth and discovered a new world, a new settlement that would become the land of the free and the home of the brave, the birthplace of democracy, equality, and freedom of the individual.

Zinn, however, looks at the historic record with the cold hard stare of a journalist who follows the creed: "If your mother says she loves you, check it out." Zinn departs from the customary nationalistic bias and tells the story not as "the discovery of the New World" by the only civilization that mattered, but as the invasion of the Americas by Europeans.

Zinn went to the source, to Columbus's own journals, letters, and reports, and the writings of Bartolomé de las Casas, a young priest who participated in Columbus's conquest of Cuba and spent forty years on Hispaniola and surrounding islands. In these records we see a very different Columbus than the one we learned of in elementary school.

Zinn acknowledges that Columbus was a skilled navigator who, like other informed people of his time, knew the earth was round. But he also shows that Columbus was an extremely brutal man on a single-minded quest for gold for his patrons, King Fernando and Queen Isabella of Spain. They had financed his trip, and they didn't do it for the glory of exploration. They wanted gold and other bounty. Columbus thought he would land in Asia and the Indies islands and promised his benefactors he would bring them gold, silk, and spices.

Though he did not yet understand the implications of the fact that he had disembarked in a land unknown to Europe, he was determined to make good on his promises.

The first people Columbus encountered when he landed in the islands now known as the Bahamas were the Arawak people. Columbus found them remarkable, not only in their physical beauty and the harmony of their social lives, but for their hospitality and generosity. He wrote admiringly of them. "They are the best people in the world, and above all the gentlest–without knowledge of what is evil–nor do they murder or steal ... they love their neighbors as themselves and they have the sweetest talk in the world ... always laughing ... They willingly traded everything they owned ... They were well-built, with good bodies and handsome features ... They do not bear arms, and do not

know of them, for I showed them a sword, they took it and cut themselves out of ignorance." Unfortunately for the Arawaks, Columbus did not mirror their generosity of spirit. He saw great opportunity to enrich his patrons in Spain. The Arawaks, he wrote, "would make fine servants. With fifty men we could subjugate them all and make them do whatever we want."

Columbus was a man of business. He had persuaded Queen Isabella of Spain to invest in his expedition on the basis of the great riches he would bring her from the Far East. Though he admired and liked the natives, he was under pressure to return with treasure from this land. Spain was one of the great nation states forming in Europe, and gold was an international currency. Fernando and Isabella agreed to give Columbus, who had been a merchant's clerk in the city of Genoa, Italy, 10 percent of his profits, governorship of the lands he discovered, and the title Admiral of the Ocean Sea.

Columbus took back glowing, exaggerated reports of what he found and was in turn outfitted by the King with seventeen ships and 1,200 men with the mission of bringing back slaves and gold. It was the beginning of a nightmarish reign of terror for the native people. Within two years, half of the island's 250,000 Indians were dead. Columbus, who considered himself a devout Catholic, wrote, "Let us in the name of the Holy Trinity go on sending all the slaves that can be sold." By 1515 there were only 50,000 Arawaks surviving; by 1550 there were five hundred; and by 1650 none of the original Arawaks or their descendants had survived.

Columbus set up 340 gallows on the island and set quotas for the natives for how much gold to bring him. If they fell short, their arms were hacked off. Those who fled were hunted down with hounds. Thousands took cassava poison to kill themselves.

The brutality of the Spanish conquerors extended beyond the acquisition of wealth to sadism for its own sake. Bartolomé de las Casas wrote of Spanish soldiers stabbing Indians for sport and crashing babies' heads on stones. His reports are corroborated by other witnesses. The Spanish reached the point where they refused to walk any distance, preferring to ride on the back of a native, or to be carried by servants on hammocks. He wrote that they "thought nothing" of knifing the native people by the tens and twenties or "cutting slices of them to test the sharpness of their blades."

Columbus was followed by many other conquerors from Europe, who exploited and slaughtered the native people of the Americas in the same manner: Cortes with the Aztecs of Mexico, Pizarro with the Incas of Peru, and the English settlers of Virginia and Massachusetts with the Powhatans and the Pequots.

Establishing an Alternative View

After blowing away the images of Columbus as a noble and benevolent hero, Zinn pauses to state very clearly why his version of history is so different. History textbooks tell the story of Columbus without the violence and greed, celebrating Columbus as a hero. A few historians mentioned the slaughter of the natives, even going so far in the case of Harvard historian Samuel Eliot Morison as to call it genocide, but still passing over it as a minor note, a single page in a multi-volume history.

Even though he acknowledges that Columbus's policies led to "complete genocide," Morison, whom Zinn calls "the most distinguished writer on Columbus," glosses over the ethical problem in favor of portraying Columbus as a hero. "He had his faults and defects," wrote Morison, "but they were largely the defects of the qualities that made him great—his indomitable will, his superb faith in God, his own mission as the Christbearer to lands beyond the seas..." As Zinn points out, this "Christ bearer" was a mass murderer.

The problem with this traditional telling of history, Zinn said, is that it sends a message that slaughter of innocents is a necessary and acceptable part of human progress, and it condones the same behavior today.

After presenting such a jarring image of Columbus, Zinn's history continues to shatter one image after another. If Columbus was not the noble hero that we have been told about, what of the greatly revered founders of the United States? Indeed, Zinn's portrayal of them is a shocking departure from the familiar stories.

Slavery and Racism

After the establishment of the North American colonies, the conquest of the New World gathered momentum and ushered in the colonial era, driven by a frenzied drive for wealth by the nation states of Europe and the rise of a new capitalist economic order. In that economic system slavery became a driving force and one of the largest industries in the world. Slavery was an international phenomenon, but there was no country, Zinn wrote, where racism was more important for as long a time as the United States. It is important, then, to look very closely at how racism began, and hopefully gain some insight into how it might finally be left behind.

The slave trade actually began fifty years before Columbus's voyage, when Portuguese traders brought ten Africans to Lisbon to be sold in bondage. In 1619 a Dutch-flagged ship pulled into the colony of Jamestown, Virginia, then only a dozen years old, with twenty slaves.

There was a great need for labor in the New World. It was extremely difficult for Europeans transplanted into the wilderness to even survive. Creating a viable colonial system that could be profitable to its sponsors in Europe required a huge amount of labor. The colonists tried enslaving the native population. But that was difficult because the Indians were in their own homeland and far better adapted to survive there than the Europeans. Poor whites were enslaved through indentured servitude, which was at its worst a form of forced labor little better than slavery. But if whites escaped, they could easier blend into the population than blacks, who were marked by their skin color. And they were still in their native culture. Black Africans could be ripped from their cultures and social support systems and thrust into a world in which they had virtually nothing to hold on to. That made them easier to enslave.

The class system of England was imported more or less intact to America. Colonial aristocrats were in positions of authority and wealth through appointments and land grants from the English crown. In fact, with survival so difficult in the New World, class lines actually hardened. The extreme difference between the few who had great riches and many who lived from day to day in a bitter struggle for survival created resentments. There were many rebellions and the landholders needed to find ways to protect themselves from the unruly masses. It was in the interest of the aristocracy to keep the lower classes divided so the poor people would not be able to realize the power they could have if they combined their energies and revolted against the minority in control.

With Indian hostility and slave revolts to contend with, the aristocrats needed to assuage the resentment of poor whites. In what was known as Bacon's Rebellion in Virginia, poor whites and blacks joined forces against the aristocracy. That put fear into the aristocracy of how badly they could be outnumbered and overrun if blacks and whites joined forces against them.

So the aristocracy intentionally fostered division among blacks, Indians, and poor whites by granting a few rights and privileges to poor whites, but still keeping them poor enough that that they would fear displacement by the even poorer and more unfortunate blacks. After Bacon's Rebellion, amnesty was given to whites who had rebelled, but not to blacks. White servants were allowed to join the Virginia militia in place of white freemen. And slave patrols were assembled, paying poor whites to police the slaves.

Revolutionary Fervor in America

The colonies in the New World were fraught with rebellions. There were eighteen uprisings against the colonial government in Virginia. By 1776 a group of the aristocratic English colonists came up with the idea of creating a nation. Through this device, Zinn writes, "they could take over land, profits, and political power from favorites of the British Empire. In the process they could hold back a number of potential rebellions and create a consensus of popular support for the rule of a new, privileged leadership." The founders, "created the most effective system of national control devised in modern times."

Britain needed money to pay off its war debts after its Seven Years War (French and Indian War), so it raised taxes on the colonies. As the colonies became more prosperous, the wealthy farmers began to feel they could function better without having England on their backs, taxing them and forcing them to sell all their produce to England at prices set by England. They began to envision an independent nation.

The colonists who joined together to create the new nation were the richest landowners of the colonies. Many, like Washington and Jefferson, were also slaveholders. A tiny minority of colonists had almost all the money and land. Land holdings granted by the British Crown had dubious legitimacy because the land was, after all, taken from the native people, usually by force or trickery. Class resentment was strong and often erupted in violence against the wealthy establishment.

The colonial aristocracy wanted to divert the class resentment away from themselves and toward the British government. They also needed to enlist the help of the common people if they had any hope of resisting the British military.

In order to establish their own rule, the aristocrats needed to grant some concessions to the middle class at the expense of those below them in social rank, including poor whites, blacks, and Indians. They used the language of equality of writers like Thomas Paine, borrowing from works of Enlightenment writers like John Stuart Mill and John Locke, and promises of some limited land or monetary rewards to entice the lower and middle classes to support them against England without having to grant them real equality.

They planned a government that would grant some limited rights to common people–a little more than they would get under British dominion——and thereby enlist their support. Their idea was to form a republic, not a democracy. When they said "all men are created equal," they referred to the landed gentry like themselves. Those without property were not to be allowed to vote. Women did not even deserve a mention. At that time under English law they were considered property, as were, of course, slaves.

Cheating the Indians

The newly formed American republic wanted to expand westward and saw the Native Americans as an obstacle, so the government devised various ways of getting them out of the way, relying primarily on trickery, broken promises, massacre, and germ warfare.

In 1790 there were 3,900,000 colonial European Americans, most living within fifty miles of the coast. By 1830 there were thirteen million, and by 1840, over four million had moved on beyond the Appalachian Mountains into the Mississippi River Valley. In 1820, 120,000 Native Americans lived east of the Mississippi River; twenty-two years later in 1844, only 30,000 were left. The colonists continued to push westward, creating much conflict with the native inhabitants, so President Jefferson committed the government to policies of Indian Removal. The government wanted to open the continent for agriculture and manufacturing for the markets of a developing capitalist economic system.

Treaties were routinely ignored. Though the Chickasaw Indians had fought on the side of the colonists against the British during the revolution, and a treaty had been signed guaranteeing them the ownership of that land, after the Revolution much of their land in North Carolina was put up for sale by the government. A state surveyor named John Donelson ended up in possession of 20,000 acres in Tennessee. His son-in-law was Andrew Jackson, a land speculator, merchant, and slave trader, whom Zinn calls "the most aggressive enemy of the Indians in early American history." Jackson emerged as a hero in the War of 1812, which Zinn points out, was not just a defense against Britain for survival of the new nation, as the story is told, but was also a struggle to expand the new nation into Florida, Canada, and Indian territory.

Jackson won recognition as a hero when he fought the Battle of Horseshoe Bend in 1814 against the Creek Indians. Though his troops had failed in a frontal attack against the Creeks, Jackson enlisted the help of Cherokee Indians by promising them good treatment by the government if they helped him. The Cherokees swam the river, attacked the Creeks from behind, and defeated them for Jackson. Jackson and his friends bought up the land seized from the Creeks. Jackson was appointed treaty commissioner, which gave him the power to make treaties with the Indians, and he created aggressive treaties to seize Indian lands, push them out, and turn their lands into farms.

In 1814 Jackson tried a new tactic for dealing with Indians, granting them individual ownership of land, which broke up the communal landholding practices of the Indians, put them in competition with each other, and led to the shattering of their culture. Jackson used the conflicts with the Seminole Indians as a pretext for invading Florida, which was at that time claimed by the Spanish. He claimed it was a sanctuary for escaped slaves and marauding Indians, so he led raids across the border, burned Indian villages, and attacked Spanish forts, eventually forcing Spain to "sell" the territory, of which Jackson then became governor. He was elected president in 1828.

The Indian Removal bill was called "the leading measure" of his administration. Under Jackson and his chosen successor Martin Van Buren, 70,000 Indians east

of the Mississippi were forced westward. The actions against the Indians were many and varied. States passed laws that made tribal meetings illegal, took away the legal status of the tribe and the authority of the chief, subjected them to taxes and military duty, but did not give them rights to vote or participate in court proceedings. They could stay if they wanted to endure harassment, the breakup of their civilization, and treatment as a subhuman species.

The movement of whites was seen as the progress of civilization. The Indians were seen as a barbarous people who could not live in contact with civilization and whose extinction was inevitable. Each time the Indians were uprooted, they would be given solemn promises that they would finally have a permanent home never to be molested again. But the promises were soon forgotten. According to historian Dale Van Every, before 1832 there is no recorded instance of a treaty that was not broken by the whites. Within a few days of the signing of the Treaty of Washington in 1832, whites invaded the newly designated Creek territory and the federal government did nothing about it, instead offering a new treaty to move the Creeks farther west.

Manifest Destiny

The idea of expanding the country to the Pacific Ocean took hold in the minds of many Americans and the push began to expand westward to California. Jefferson arranged the Louisiana Purchase from France, which doubled the size of the U.S. Then the government set its focus on Mexico, which held much of the territory between the Louisiana Purchase and the Pacific Ocean. Mexico had won its independence from Spain in a revolutionary war in 1821. Its territory included Texas and the territory that is now New Mexico, Utah, Nevada, Arizona, California, and part of Colorado.

Some Texans, with support of the U.S. government, had declared themselves independent of Mexico. In 1845 Congress declared Texas a state. When President James K. Polk took office, he told his Secretary of the Navy that taking control of California was one of his main objectives. He started by moving troops to the Rio Grande, within the territory of Mexico, as a provocation. In early 1846, some soldiers disappeared and one was found dead. Then a patrol of soldiers was attacked and sixteen were killed. Polk had been trying to get Congress to give him a declaration of war based on some financial matters, or of "imminent danger" of violence because Polk had sent troops into Mexican territory. But once the violent incidents had taken place, all restraints were dropped. The Senate limited its debate on the war resolution to one day. The Whigs put up some objections to the war, but they supported the expansion and all the measures for appropriations of funds for the war.

Abraham Lincoln was elected to Congress in 1846 with the war already in progress. Lincoln opposed the war and introduced a "spot resolution" in which he challenged Polk to say on which spot the incident had occurred. But he would not go so far as to vote against the appropriations of men and supplies for the war.

War fervor grew, rallies in support of the war took place in major cities, and thousands rushed to volunteer as soldiers. Opposition to the war also took shape. Abolitionists opposed the war. The American Anti-Slavery Society objected that the war was being waged to extend slavery into the soon-to-be-annexed territory of Mexico. The poet James Russell Lowell wrote poems against the war for the *Boston Courier* and they became known as the *Biglow Papers*. Henry David Thoreau refused to pay his poll tax as a protest against the war and was put in jail for one night. But his

friends paid the tax and he was released. Two years later he summarized his beliefs on noncompliance with unjust laws in an essay called "Civil Disobedience." Ralph Waldo Emerson also wrote against the war, as did Frederick Douglass, the former slave. Irish workers in New York, Boston, and Lowell, Massachusetts, demonstrated against the war.

People enlisted in the army for money and social advancement. Half of the army was made up of immigrants, mostly from Germany and Ireland. Many reported being tricked into signing up while under the influence of alcohol, or false promises. The patriotic fervor whipped up to launch the war soon faded. Meanwhile the killing, robbing, raping, and pillaging of war raged on as American armies marched across Mexican territory to the Pacific

Ocean and claimed California for the United States. In a war between U.S. elites and Mexican elites, soldiers were being killed by their enemies and even by men on their own side. Battles were fought with no military objective, and thus civilians, women, and children were killed in great numbers. Volunteers rebelled and nine thousand of them deserted. Finally Mexico surrendered and the U.S. took half its territory.

The Battle Over Slavery

Slaves did not submit willingly to their bondage and forced labor. Slaveholders had an ongoing problem trying to maintain control, keep hold of the slaves, and make them work. The problems got worse as the black community became more and more determined to achieve freedom.

By 1860 the south was producing a million tons of cotton each year and there were four million slaves, up from 500,000 only seventy years before. The control of the slave population was achieved mostly due to harshly brutal treatment bolstered by laws, courts, the military, and the racial prejudice entrenched in society. But the system was inherently vulnerable to the resistance of a freedom-seeking people as well as non-slaves who recognized the injustice of slavery.

Families were torn apart. Slaves were whipped, beaten, and worked hard, but there was always the possibility of escape, disobedience, or outright rebellion. Rebellion took place on many levels, from small acts of defiance, to some noteworthy large-scale rebellions. In New Orleans in 1811, four to five hundred slaves gathered at the plantation of a Major Andry armed with cane knives, axes, and clubs. They wounded Andry and killed his son, then went on a rampage from plantation to plantation, gathering more supporters as they went. The U.S. army and militia forces went after them, killed sixty-six on the scene, and tried sixteen before sentencing them to death by firing squad. In spite of the consequences, four out of five slaves engaged in some sort of disobedience.

Enslaved blacks developed alternative support systems. To compensate for their families being torn apart, they developed extended family kinship networks and supported each other. Slaves took the first opportunity to escape, many of them joining the Union army when the Civil War began. Pressure mounted against the slavery system from within and without. Late in the war when the Confederacy was desperate, some southern leaders proposed releasing slaves and using them as soldiers. In early 1865, Confederate President Jefferson Davis signed a Negro Soldier Law authorizing the enlistment of blacks as soldiers. But before it could take effect, the war was over.

When Lincoln issued the Emancipation Proclamation, saying that slaves were freed by the federal government, it was seen by many as an order coming down from above rather than the act of slaves freeing themselves. It could therefore be controlled, dictated, and limited from above.

After the war, a congressional law approved by Lincoln returned the confiscated land in the South to the heirs of the plantation owners. Some blacks complained that the compensation should have gone to the slaves, who had worked the land, not to the masters, who had perpetrated the crime of slavery. After being legally freed, few ex-slaves had land or means for making a living. As a result, many returned to work for their former masters through sharecropping arrangements that kept them in debt and gave them little more freedom or empowerment than they had had under slavery.

Class Struggle in the Nineteenth Century

Most interpretations of American history put the Civil War in the spotlight as one of the major events in the life of the republic and devote a great deal of time to the minutiae of the war, its battles, and political struggles. But Zinn isn't most historians. He leaves the well-covered ground of Civil War history to others. Instead, he looks at aspects of American life that are invisible in most of the traditional history books. In Zinn's vision of history, America was the scene of class struggles growing out of a class structure imported from Europe. But the class struggles were played out on a new stage on a new frontier where capitalism was developing and creating a new world.

The Dutch colonies in the 1600s had been ruled under a system of patronship, a sort of feudal system in which a few landlords controlled all the land and rented parcels out to many tenants, ruling over the lives of hundreds of thousands of people. In the 1800s the social structure of patronship was still evident in a residual form. But rebellion against the old order was stirring in the form of the Anti-Rent movement, fueled by the ideas of freedom and equality aroused by the Enlightenment and the rhetoric

of the American Revolution. After the economic crisis of 1837 left many unemployed and broke, tenants began to organize against the landlords for better deals. Renters petitioned the legislature for a law that would protect them from being evicted. But the legislature defeated the bill. Tensions mounted and violence erupted. Rebels were put down and dealt with harshly, told that their rebellion had to be enforced through acceptable channels, such as voting, which only landowners could do. So the energy of rebellion was diverted into a drive to expand the right to vote.

In Rhode Island the struggle for voting rights took the form of Dorr's Rebellion, led by Thomas Dorr, a lawyer. In 1841 thousands paraded in Providence calling for a broadening of voting rights. They organized a People's Convention and wrote their own constitution without property qualifications for voting. They held an election on their constitution, which was endorsed by a majority of the population, including a majority of the landholders who were legally allowed to vote. The rebels formed their own People's Legislature. Though Dorr himself objected, the new constitution did not

extend voting rights to blacks, which angered blacks and caused them to join the side of government militia that was putting down the rebellion. Dorr was imprisoned for twenty months then freed by a newly elected governor who wanted to end Dorr's martyrdom. The Dorr movement took its case to the Supreme Court, claiming to be the legitimate government of Rhode Island, but the Supreme Court sided with the establishment.

With tensions created by the growing pains of a rapidly evolving society, the growth of the factory system and continued influx of immigrants, the government needed a mass base of support, and Jacksonian Democracy, as it was called, created the means for achieving it.

THE PEOPLE, OH, YEAH, WOULDN'T BE HERE WITHOUT 'EM.

In the 1830s and 1840s Jackson was able to enlist the support of a broad base of the population by projecting the image of a man of the people. He was the first to master the liberal rhetoric and make the common man believe he spoke for them, and was one of them. He appealed to farmers, laborers, mechanics, professionals and businessmen without ever having to reveal his position on a variety of vital issues. He was not clearly for or against labor, business, or any class. Even though he had sent troops to break a strike on the Chesapeake and Ohio Canal, he received the backing of organized labor.

New forms of control were needed as the country grew and developed rapidly. It was at this time that the two-party system became established, which allowed the public to choose between one or the other, one perhaps more democratic than the other, but both representing wings of the establishment. Jackson won support by providing a little reform, but not enough to upset the established order.

From 1790 to 1840 the population of the cities grew from fewer than one million to eleven million. People were packed together and the poor lived in crowded and difficult circumstances. In Philadelphia, fifty-five families shared a tenement, one family to a room. In New York City, poor people lay in the streets among the garbage. They were a potential danger to the government if they rose up in anger, but the better paid workers and landowners could be counted on to support the government.

Capitalism developed chaotically. In Zinn's view, because it was based strictly on the profit motive without regard to the actual needs of people and society it produced periodic slumps. The big capitalists tried to secure stability by reducing competition through consolidating businesses toward more monopolization. With this in mind, there were many mergers in the mid-1850s.

Although the working class began to develop class consciousness and organize, most of that resistance is lost to history. Trades organized themselves into trade unions for the strength of collective bargaining. There were meetings, strikes, uprisings, and riots. During the Civil War there were riots against the draft and desertions on both sides as many became dissatisfied and suspected they were fighting a war between elites of both sides.

The Union fought the war not to end slavery but to retain the southern territory for markets and resources, but there was a period after the war when the anti-slavery movement achieved enough momentum to reverse some of the conditions of slavery. The Thirteenth Amendment to the Constitution outlawed slavery. The Fourteenth repudiated the Dred Scott decision that had called slaves property and established that all people born or naturalized in the U.S. were citizens. For a while the Union army stayed in the South, protecting the slaves from re-enslavement.

But after Lincoln was assassinated, he was replaced by the southerner Andrew Johnson, who was much more sympathetic with southern wishes to re-establish the old order of the southern aristocracy. Johnson dragged his feet on enforcing anti-slavery measures and started to restore the old system of white domination. He vetoed bills that were designed to help the freed blacks and made it easy for southern states to be accepted into the Union without guaranteeing rights for slaves. Southern states passed "black codes" that made the status of blacks almost as bad as when they were slaves. One of them, for example, forbid blacks from owning or leasing land and made them work under harsh labor contracts they must uphold or face imprisonment.

AH, IMPEACH ME WHY DON'CHA. HUH...

Robber Barons and the Rise of Corporate America

The Civil War set the stage for the expansion of the U.S. to a continental empire. The war fueled production and provided a jumpstart for the capitalist economy. After the Union was saved, the race was on to spread the empire to the Pacific Ocean. The war and the westward expansion helped the Robber Barons, the new supercapitalists, create their empires and build the infrastructure of what grew into the corporate America of the twenty-first century.

In the thirty-five years following the Civil War, steam and electricity augmented human labor, and wood was supplanted by iron, which was in turn supplanted by steel produced by the new Bessemer process. Industrialization grew like wildfire. Multiple innovations were changing the way Americans lived and worked.

The railroad empires were built on land grants obtained through the political system. The Central Pacific started building from the West Coast. The company paid five hundred thousand dollars in bribes in Washington to get nine million acres of free land and twenty-four million dollars in bonds. The Union Pacific started in Nebraska heading west. It was given twelve million acres of land and 27 million dollars in government bonds. The Central Pacific got the work done with three thousand Irish and ten thousand Chinese immigrants who were paid a dollar or two a day. The Union Pacific hired twenty thousand war veterans and Irish immigrants. They laid five miles of track a day and died by the hundreds from the back-breaking work and exposure to the elements. In 1869 the two lines met in Utah.

Because of the widespread fraud in the railroad industry, the railroads increasingly fell under control of the banks. By the 1890s, the railroad industry had developed into six large systems, with four of them partly or wholly controlled by the House of Morgan. The other two were controlled by Kuhn, Loeb & Company.

The son of a banker, J.P. Morgan had cut his teeth on selling railroad stocks. During the Civil War he bought five thousand rifles from an army arsenal for $3.50 each and sold them to a general for $22 each. Through smart political negotiating, his firm, Drexel, Morgan & Company, received a sweetheart government contract to float a bond issue of $260 million, which would earn it $5 million in commissions; the government could have avoided paying this sum by issuing the bonds itself. The railroads were granted miles of free land around the tracks they built. The control of the arteries of commerce and much of the land around them gave the railroads the leverage to control the economic fortunes of vast reaches of the country.

Three companies, Drexel, Morgan & Company; Kidder, Peabody & Company and Brown Brothers & Company practically controlled the rail system of the United States. They met secretly to set prices and form pacts that eliminated competition.

Other industries followed similar models to create future empires. These tactics involved shrewd and ruthless practices that made clever use of government subsidies. One industry after another fell under the control of small groups of corporations controlled in turn by banks in tight, interlocking networks of power.

John D. Rockefeller decided that whoever controlled the refineries would control the oil industry. By 1899 his Standard Oil Company controlled many other companies, and the Rockefeller fortune climbed to two billion dollars. The Rockefeller family continues to be a major force in America in the twenty-first Century.

While in London, Andrew Carnegie found out about the Bessemer method of producing steel, and the former Wall Street broker returned to the U.S. to build a steel plant. Congress protected him from foreign competition by imposing tariffs on foreign products, and as a result, Carnegie was soon making forty million dollars a year. He sold his steel company to J.P. Morgan for $492 million, enabling Morgan to form U.S. Steel.

Though the Fourteenth Amendment was designed to protect the rights of newly freed slaves, once it became law, corporate lawyers began devising ways to use it to transfer rights and power from people to corporations. By legal sleight of hand, corporations were granted the rights of human beings.

Big business ran the country and in large measure controlled the government. The need for labor was supplied by a plentiful supply of immigrants, who worked for little money and often in barely survivable conditions. Typical was the story of an Italian who was told he was going to Connecticut to work on the railroad and instead ended up in the South working in sulfate mines, kept in line by armed guards, given little food, and earning only enough money to get to work. Widespread misery led to rebellions and civil strife.

In 1893, after decades of industrial growth, manipulation of financial markets, speculation, and profiteering, the financial system collapsed in a major crisis, with 642 banks and 16,000 businesses failing. Millions were out of work. Workers and farmers rose up in anger against the big business interests. Laborers joined together in unions. Farmers combined to form alliances. In 1877 the Socialist Labor Party was formed. A working class consciousness grew. The farmers alliances joined together and became the Peoples party, or Populist party. Meeting at a Populist convention in Topeka, Kansas, in 1890, Populist Mary Ellen Lease told the crowd, "Wall Street owns the country. It is no longer a government of the people, by the people, and for the people, but a government of Wall Street... Our laws are the output of a system which clothes rascals in robes and honesty in rags..."

The Populist party grew stronger, but eventually was absorbed into the Democratic party. In 1896 the Populist/Democratic candidate, William Jennings Bryan was defeated by William McKinley, who was supported by a mobilization of major corporations and the press. McKinley struggled to contain the rebellion against the system, and after two years in office came upon a formula for arousing support of the masses. The U.S. declared war on Spain.

The Rise of American Empire

At the end of the nineteenth century, the United States reached to the Pacific coast. In one hectic century the European immigrants had rushed across the continent and claimed dominion of everything in their path. But capitalism, with its inherent principle of expansion, was not satisfied. It needed more markets, more sources of raw materials for industry. As U.S. Navy Captain A.T. Mahan, a propagandist for expansionism said, "Americans must now begin to look outward."

A *Washington Post* editorial on the eve of the Spanish American War said, "A new consciousness seems to have come upon us—the consciousness of strength—and with it a new appetite, the yearning to show our strength. ... Ambition, interest, land hunger, pride, the mere joy of fighting, whatever it may be, we are animated by a new sensation. The taste of Empire is in the mouth of the people even as the taste of blood in the jungle."

Was it really an instinctive urge for aggression, Zinn asked, or was it stirred up by "the millionaire press, the military, the government, the eager-to-please scholars of the time?"

The philosopher William James wrote that Teddy Roosevelt "gushes over war as the ideal condition of human society, for the manly strenuousness which it involves..." But Roosevelt was also very conscious of war as a way of furthering business through overseas markets. Military domination of foreign markets was referred to as the "open door policy." It sounded friendly and civilized, but if that didn't work, "the big stick" was always close at hand.

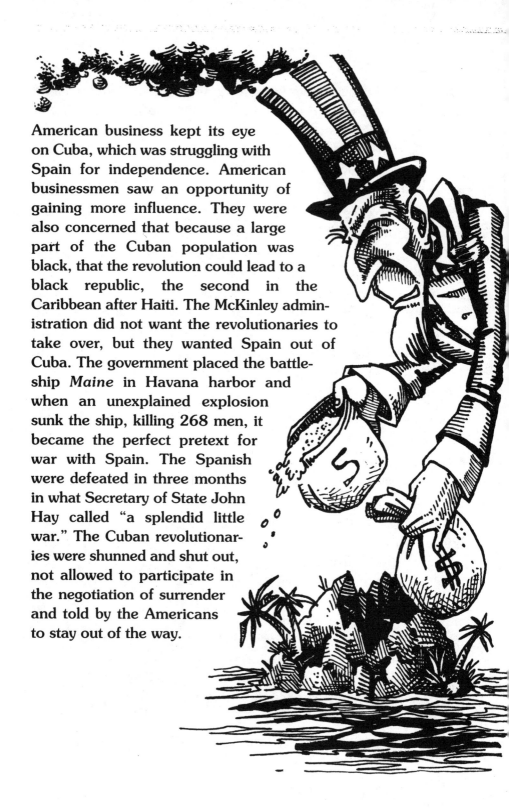

American business kept its eye on Cuba, which was struggling with Spain for independence. American businessmen saw an opportunity of gaining more influence. They were also concerned that because a large part of the Cuban population was black, that the revolution could lead to a black republic, the second in the Caribbean after Haiti. The McKinley administration did not want the revolutionaries to take over, but they wanted Spain out of Cuba. The government placed the battleship *Maine* in Havana harbor and when an unexplained explosion sunk the ship, killing 268 men, it became the perfect pretext for war with Spain. The Spanish were defeated in three months in what Secretary of State John Hay called "a splendid little war." The Cuban revolutionaries were shunned and shut out, not allowed to participate in the negotiation of surrender and told by the Americans to stay out of the way.

Though Congress had prohibited the colonization of Cuba, American businesses flocked in, taking over the lumber, sugar, mining, and railroad industries. United Fruit bought 1.9 million acres of land at twenty cents an acre and took over the sugar industry. The American Tobacco Company moved in. Eighty percent of Cuba's minerals were in the hands of American companies, mostly Bethlehem Steel.

The U.S. government told the Cuba Constitutional Convention that its army would not leave Cuba until the Platt amendment of the U.S. Congress was incorporated into the Cuban Constitution. The provision gave the U.S. the right to intervene "for the preservation of Cuban independence, the maintenance of a government adequate for the protection of life, property, and individual liberty."

Though Cuba was not officially taken over, as General Leonard Wood wrote to Teddy Roosevelt, "There is, of course, little or no independence left Cuba under the Platt Amendment." The U.S. did take over Puerto Rico, Hawaii, Guam, and the Philippines. Filipinos rose up against American domination and the U.S. fought brutally for four years to put them down, leaving thousands of Filipinos dead.

William James joined with other intellectuals, politicians, and businesspeople to form the Anti-Imperialist League to oppose the overseas exploits of the government. While the struggle raged in the Philippines, the political struggle over it raged at home.

Enter Socialism

Warfare and the stirring of patriotic emotions could only go so far in uniting and pacifying a nation, and discontent boiled up to the surface in the early twentieth century. Acclaimed writers were among those who criticized the capitalist system, including Mark Twain, Jack London, Upton Sinclair, Theodore Dreiser, and Frank Norris.

Jack London, known mostly for adventure stories like *The Call of the Wild,* was a passionate socialist who had worked his way up from poverty as the son of an unwed mother. He had experienced the hardships of life on the bottom rungs of society; he was clubbed, beaten, and tortured by police, arrested for vagrancy, and hopped freights with hoboes. But he also read Tolstoy, Flaubert, and Marx. He spent time in the slums of London and wrote a nonfiction piece about it called *People of the Abyss.* Later he wrote *The Iron Heel,* which described how fascism could take over America. "In the face of the facts that modern man lives more wretchedly than the cave-man, and that his producing power is a thousand times greater than that of the cave-man, no other conclusion is possible than that the capitalist class has mismanaged ... criminally and selfishly mismanaged." The people should take over the machines and run them themselves, he said. "That, gentlemen, is socialism."

With widespread discontent over nearly unlivable conditions of much of the population, the ideas of socialism spread and the trade union movement grew with the realization that working people could stop the system by stopping work. It was not welcomed by the capitalists, however, and the resulting war on the streets became extremely brutal.

At the outset unions were practically all white and all male, and there was a great deal of racism within the unions, as those on the bottom struggled to hold on to whatever they could. They were turned against each other by those who owned and controlled production. As the largest union, the American Federation of Labor, grew larger and more powerful, it also became corrupt as its upper echelon became accustomed to the privileges of wealth and rank. In 1905, two hundred socialists, anarchists, and radical trade unionists met in Chicago to form a new kind of union, the Industrial Workers of the World (IWW). It came together for "emancipation of the working class from the slave bondage of capitalism" and to put the "working class in possession of the economic power, the means of life, in control of the machinery of production and distribution, without regard to the capitalist masters." Among the founders were Eugene V. Debs, leader of the Socialist party, and Mother Mary Jones, a seventy-five-year-old organizer for the United Mine Workers.

The IWW members ("Wobblies") wanted to combine all unions into one big union, inclusive of all, no longer keeping out women or blacks. They did not initiate violence, but did fight back when attacked. They learned from the ideas of anarcho-syndicalism that were growing in Italy, Spain, and France, summarized in the words of IWW organizer Joseph Ettor: "If the workers of the world want to win, all they have to do is recognize their own solidarity. They have nothing to do but fold their arms and the world will stop."

119

But the owners were willing to employ their own armies of thugs to enforce their will upon workers and there were many grim incidents. Joe Hill, an IWW organizer, was a songwriter who created songs that became anthems of the movement. In 1915 he was accused of killing a grocer in a robbery in Salt Lake City. Though there was no direct evidence, there was enough circumstantial evidence to convince a jury, and he was executed by firing squad in spite of 10,000 letters to the governor in protest. Many demonstrations were attacked by police and thugs; people were clubbed, beaten, kicked, blackjacked, shot, tortured, and hung. By 1904 there were 4,000 strikes a year.

To quiet things down, government introduced reforms, leading to the adoption of the term "the Progressive Period." The reforms were focused on calming the uprisings, without making fundamental changes. Under President Theodore Roosevelt, laws were passed to enforce regulate railroads and pipelines, food and drugs, telephone and telegraph systems, and the banking system. Though the reforms did not threaten the status quo, they dropped enough of the wealth of the ruling classes into the working classes to calm down the unrest and to create a buffer between the top and bottom levels of society.

The reforms also strengthened the power of central government and enabled businessmen to exercise more control over government. Business favored the reforms because they initiated stability to the troubled capitalist system. Roosevelt became known as a trust-buster. His successor, the conservative William Howard Taft, actually busted more trusts than Roosevelt.

The Warfare State

In a society run by capitalism, with periodic slumps and crashes, with vast distances between the fortunes of the rich and the destitution of the poor, and rebellion boiling up from the bottom, war serves many purposes. It creates markets and spikes production, giving the economy a jumpstart and enriching industries. It ignites patriotism, diverts dissent, and creates justifications for actions that would be unacceptable in peace time.

Soon after the turn of the twentieth century, a long period of relative peace, prosperity, and progress in the western world came to a close as The Great War ignited in Europe and blazed for months turning into years. Ten million died in battle and twenty million more died of hunger and disease resulting from the war. Thousands died just to move the battle lines a few yards one way or the other.

121

And, Zinn says, no one can show any purpose for it, anything that was accomplished for humanity.

Socialists called it an imperialist war, with the advanced capitalist countries fighting over territory, resources, colonies, and spheres of influence. President Woodrow Wilson campaigned for re-election in 1916 on having "kept us out of war," but after taking office, he brought America into the war.

To provide a legal justification for entering the war, Wilson focused on the German announcement that they would attack ships that brought supplies to their enemies. Wilson said he could not consent to any "abridgement of the rights of American citizens" and then plunged them into the European catastrophe.

The U.S. had gone into recession in 1914, but supplying war materials for the allies had become a good market for American business and helped bolster a failing economy. Wilson had declared that America needed markets abroad, and The Great War created a big one. W.E.B. Du Bois wrote that American capitalism needed international rivalry and periodic war to create an artificial community between rich and poor and divert the actual community of interest of the poor that tended to erupt in political action.

Wilson's biographer wrote that the war was determined by Wilson "and public opinion," but Zinn argues that public support for the war had to be artificially churned up with a massive propaganda campaign. There were so few volunteers—only 73,000 of the one million the government hoped for—that Congress was forced to institute a draft.

After Congress declared war, the Socialist party grew in strength, with thousands turning up whenever Socialists gave speeches. Congress passed the Espionage Act to suppress dissent. It mandated prison terms of up to twenty years for people who attempted "to cause insubordination, disloyalty, mutiny, or refusal of duty in the military or naval forces." It was used to intimidate and imprison people who spoke or wrote against the war. In 1918 Socialist leader Eugene Debs gave a speech across the street from a jail that held three Socialists for resisting the draft. He was arrested under the Espionage Act and sentenced to ten years in prison. He served thirty-two months and in 1921, at age sixty-six, was released by President Warren G. Harding. About 900 people served time under the Espionage Act out of 2,000 prosecutions.

The *New York Times* ran an editorial in 1917 that said, "It is the duty of every good citizen to communicate to proper authorities any evidence of sedition that comes to his notice." The Post Office Department took away mailing privileges from publications that printed antiwar articles. In Los Angeles, a film was shown about the American Revolution called *The Spirit of '76,* which portrayed atrocities committed by British troops on American colonists. The filmmaker was prosecuted under the Espionage Act because, according to the judge, the film questioned "the good faith of our ally Great Britain."

The war ended in 1919 with 50,000 Americans dead. When it was over, the threat of socialism still loomed over the elite classes. In 1920 a typesetter and anarchist named Andrea Salsedo was arrested by FBI agents and held for eight weeks on the 14th floor of the Park Row Building in New York, prohibited from contacting anyone. When his crushed body was found on the pavement below, the FBI said he had committed suicide. After Salsedo's death, two of his friends, Nicola Sacco and Bartolomeo Vanzetti, started carrying guns. They were arrested on a streetcar and accused of committing a holdup and murder at a shoe factory. They were convicted and sentenced to death. After seven years of appeals they were electrocuted.

Hard Times USA

When the Great War ended, strikes broke out all over America. A strike of 35,000 shipyard workers spread into a general strike of 100,000 in Seattle and brought the city to a standstill. Strikes and disruptions spread from industry to industry, but by the 1920s, the leadership of the International Workers of the World had been jailed and the organization was destroyed. The Socialist party was falling apart. The boom of the '20s reduced unemployment and prosperity rose, though only the upper 10 percent achieved a substantial increase in income. Protests and disruptions died down and those that took place were not widely reported by the big media companies that largely controlled the movement of information in the country.

The story that was not being told in the mainstream press was left to writers like Theodore Dreiser, Sinclair Lewis, and F. Scott Fitzgerald. In "Echoes of the Jazz Age" Fitzgerald wrote of the "upper tenth of the nation living with the insouciance of a grand duc and the casualness of chorus girls." Sinclair Lewis wrote of the shallow falseness of the new prosperity in his novel *Babbit*. In 1929 came the stock market crash and the Great Depression, brought on by wild speculation that collapsed and took the economy down with it. From Zinn's point of view, the capitalist system was fundamentally unsound because it was driven entirely by the drive for corporate profit. It was an ineffective principle by which to direct a society.

When the stock market crashed, the country was stunned and unable to get moving again. Five thousand banks closed, money stopped circulating, and without access to cash, businesses folded in droves. Those in authority had no clue what to do about it. President Herbert Hoover remained in denial of the problem. Just before the crash he had said that America was nearing the final triumph over poverty. When the depression set in, he kept saying it would soon end. There was plenty of food and clothing and other goods around, but it was not profitable to distribute it or sell it, so it stayed where it was. Houses stood empty because people couldn't afford to move into them. Shantytowns grew where homeless people gathered, and they became known as "Hoovervilles."

Homeless veterans of the Great War gathered in Washington, D.C, to persuade Congress to pay them for government bonus certificates they had received for their service. The bonds were not yet due, but the veterans needed money. More than 20,000 of them camped out across the Potomac River from the Capitol. Some stayed in deserted government buildings,

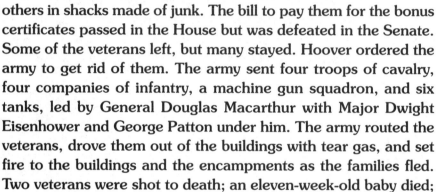

others in shacks made of junk. The bill to pay them for the bonus certificates passed in the House but was defeated in the Senate. Some of the veterans left, but many stayed. Hoover ordered the army to get rid of them. The army sent four troops of cavalry, four companies of infantry, a machine gun squadron, and six tanks, led by General Douglas Macarthur with Major Dwight Eisenhower and George Patton under him. The army routed the veterans, drove them out of the buildings with tear gas, and set fire to the buildings and the encampments as the families fled. Two veterans were shot to death; an eleven-week-old baby died; and an eight-year-old boy was partially blinded, and a thousand veterans were injured by tear gas.

In 1932 Hoover was massively defeated by Franklin D. Roosevelt, who came into office with broad-ranging reforms designed to reorganize and bolster capitalism and stem the tide of rebellion. Through a series of initiatives, many were put to work. The National Recovery Act was dominated by big business. The Agricultural Adjustment Administration favored the big farming enterprises. Unemployment and dire poverty remained widespread, and they led to many incidents of violence and disruption. In 1934 the Wagner Act was passed to regulate labor disputes.

Some observers said that the spontaneous sit-down strikes were more effective than those organized by union leadership. In 1936 there were 48 sit-down strikes. The next year there were 477. The National Labor Relations Board gave the unions legal status, which moderated the struggles by channeling energy into elections. The system responded to rebellions by devising new methods of control.

World War II: The Clash of Empires

When fascism, the extreme perversion of predatory capitalism, began its march across Europe, it created a threat that united even the Communists with the Allied Powers. The fascists represented a truly evil threat. But once the war was on, it was not simply a battle between good and evil.

The U.S. did not enter the war to save the Jews from Hitler any more than it had fought the Civil War to free the slaves, Zinn says. Business continued as usual, with American companies continuing to supply the axis countries with the supplies they needed to perpetrate their attacks. American oil companies sent oil to Italy to fuel its invasion of Ethiopia. When rebellion broke out against fascism in Spain, Roosevelt sponsored a neutrality act that gave Spain's dictator Franco a free hand, with the help of Hitler and

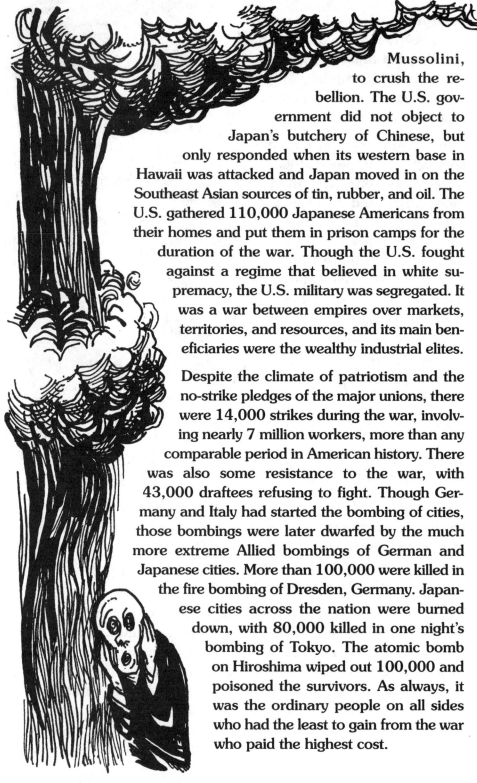

Mussolini, to crush the rebellion. The U.S. government did not object to Japan's butchery of Chinese, but only responded when its western base in Hawaii was attacked and Japan moved in on the Southeast Asian sources of tin, rubber, and oil. The U.S. gathered 110,000 Japanese Americans from their homes and put them in prison camps for the duration of the war. Though the U.S. fought against a regime that believed in white supremacy, the U.S. military was segregated. It was a war between empires over markets, territories, and resources, and its main beneficiaries were the wealthy industrial elites.

Despite the climate of patriotism and the no-strike pledges of the major unions, there were 14,000 strikes during the war, involving nearly 7 million workers, more than any comparable period in American history. There was also some resistance to the war, with 43,000 draftees refusing to fight. Though Germany and Italy had started the bombing of cities, those bombings were later dwarfed by the much more extreme Allied bombings of German and Japanese cities. More than 100,000 were killed in the fire bombing of Dresden, Germany. Japanese cities across the nation were burned down, with 80,000 killed in one night's bombing of Tokyo. The atomic bomb on Hiroshima wiped out 100,000 and poisoned the survivors. As always, it was the ordinary people on all sides who had the least to gain from the war who paid the highest cost.

The U.S. insisted on unconditional surrender from the Japanese. If U.S. authorities had agreed on one condition—that the emperor, who was considered holy to the Japanese, would remain in place—the surrender would have taken place much earlier. As it was, the Japanese were on the verge of surrender, without an invasion of the Japanese mainland. The American authorities, who had broken the Japanese code, knew it. The Russians had agreed to declare war on Japan ninety days after the war in Europe ended, which would have been August 8, 1945. The Hiroshima bomb was dropped August 6. The second bomb, dropped on Nagasaki, was a plutonium bomb instead of a uranium bomb. It was scheduled in advance and went forward in spite of the fact that Japan was on the verge of collapse. Zinn wonders whether the second bomb was dropped as an experiment.

Even before World War II was over, the ground was already laid for the Cold War, the struggle between the West and Communism. Anti-Communist panic spread through the U.S., leading to McCarthyism, which used the Senate as a forum for accusing large parts of the population of being Communists.

The arms industry, which had been the economic driver that finally pulled the U.S. out of the depression, was kept intact after the war. The Cold War was used to justify the arms expenditures and the military draft, while it also kept the population in line by rallying them against a common enemy. The ever-increasing military expenditures became like a drug addiction with corporations competing for their share of the bounty. As President Eisenhower, a former general, warned against in his farewell address, the maintenance of a peacetime military production industry led to unwarranted influence of the industry on government policy.

The Black Revolution

To those Americans well entrenched in conventional belief systems of a racially segregated society, the outbreak of a rebellion of African Americans in the 1950s and 1960s was a surprise. But the suffering and indignation of an enslaved people was always evident to those who really looked. The discontent was expressed eloquently in literature going back at least to Mark Twain's *Huckleberry Finn* and Harriet Beecher Stowe's *Uncle Tom's Cabin* in the nineteenth century, and increasingly by black writers throughout the twentieth century, such as Langston Hughes, Claude McKay, Paul Laurence Dunbar, Margaret Walker, Richard Wright, W.E.B. Du Bois, and many others who followed. The social system that kept one race in a permanently inferior position was a hot issue constantly on the verge of igniting.

Black militancy made appearances in the 1930s, but moved into the background during World War II. In the postwar environment, with the Soviet Union presenting a rival system to the world, American leaders became concerned that the perception of the United States as an oppressive country, hypocritical in its pronouncement of human rights, would undermine its image and make Communism look good. The movements for self-determination of Third World people began to adopt Marxist language. In 1946 President Harry Truman appointed a Commission on Civil Rights, which recommended expanding laws against lynching, voter discrimination, and job discrimination. There were moral reasons for it, the committee said, but there were also economic reasons. Discrimination was a waste of money and resources and was damaging America in world politics. Truman had a challenge from the left with the Progressive Party in the election of 1948, and four months after the election, he issued an executive order to de-segregate the military "as rapidly as possible." It took 10 years.

WELL, WHAT MORALITY DOESN'T LEAD YOU TO DO EXPEDIENCY WILL.

In 1954 the Supreme Court struck down the "separate but equal" doctrine that had stood since the late nineteenth century, but did not specify a time limit. A year later it issued another ruling that it should be done "with all deliberate speed." Ten years later, 75 percent of the school districts in the south were still segregated. But in the mid-'50s, blacks in the south began to agitate to make the changes in law into realities in their lives.

In Montgomery, Alabama, in 1955, a 43-year-old black seamstress named Rosa Parks refused to obey the rule that blacks had to sit at the back of bus and was arrested. Blacks in Montgomery called a meeting and voted to boycott the city buses. The city responded by indicting one hundred leaders of the boycott and sent many of them to jail. White supremacists reacted in an explosion of violence, setting off bombs in four black churches, firing a shotgun into the door and then bombing the home of Martin Luther King, Jr., one of the organizers. King held to the principle of nonviolent resistance, as taught by Ghandi, and it proved to be very effective. Violence was something the power structure was well equipped to deal with. Nonviolent resistance perplexed them. And with the eyes of the world increasingly turned upon the movement, their violence began to work against them.

But the authorities refused to enforce laws against discrimination and segregation, or defend those in the movement, and many blacks lost patience with nonviolence. The progress was still largely a matter of words and pronouncements, with little visible progress in people's lives. Though nonviolent resistance still prevailed in general, some refused to take violent assaults without responding. Two years into the movement that began with the Rosa Parks incident, a former marine named Robert Williams who headed the NAACP chapter in Monroe, North Carolina, made known his views that blacks should defend themselves when attacked. When Klansmen attacked of one of the leaders of the NAACP, Williams and others returned fire.

A group called the Congress of Racial Equality organized Freedom Rides to challenge segregated seating on interstate buses. It had been illegal since 1947, but in 1961 the president, now John F. Kennedy, was still reluctant to offend southern politicians by taking action. The Freedom Riders were attacked with fists, iron bars, and clubs. A bus was set on fire in Alabama. Riders were jailed. The FBI took notes, but no action. The police did not step in to stop the violence. Attorney General Robert F. Kennedy did not insist on compliance with the law, but rather cut a deal with Mississippi authorities to let the Freedom Riders be arrested in return for police protection against mob violence.

But in spite of the brutal reaction, the movement was persistent and gathered momentum and support from a widening circle of people, white and black, from the north as well as the south, and around the world. They faced formidable resistance. In Birmingham in 1963 thousands of blacks demonstrated in the streets, facing police clubs and dogs, tear gas, and high-powered water hoses. The Department of Justice noted 1,412 demonstrations in three months in 1963. And the world was watching.

When Kennedy learned of the massive March on Washington planned for the summer of 1963, he endorsed it and it became a friendly affair during which Martin Luther King, Jr. gave his "I Have a Dream" speech. John Lewis, a leader of SNCC, was asked to tone down his speech by the leaders of the march. Eighteen days after the event, a black church in Birmingham was

bombed, killing four Sunday school girls. Many blacks were no longer satisfied with friendly talk combined with refusal to take action to defend their lives. The militant tones of Malcolm X found a wider audience. Malcolm said that when Kennedy endorsed the March on Washington, he took it over and it ceased to be angry. It became more like a picnic, a circus complete with clowns. "You'll get your freedom by letting your enemy know you'll do anything to get your freedom; then you'll get it," he said. "It's the only way you'll get it."

In June 1964, members of the movement rented a theater not far from the White House and brought in blacks from Mississippi to testify about the dangers they faced. Constitutional lawyers testified on the government's legal authority and its mandate to take action against the violence. A transcript of the event was delivered to President Johnson and Attorney General Robert Kennedy. Neither responded. Twelve days after the meeting one black and two white civil rights workers were arrested in Mississippi, released from jail in the middle of the night, then beaten with chains and shot dead. Some of the killers later served jail sentences, but to many blacks, the murders were a deadly reminder of the way in which the federal government passively encouraged the murderous actions of segregationists.

In 1965 President Johnson sponsored and Congress passed a Voting Rights Law that promised federal protection of the right to vote. As Johnson was signing it, an incident broke out in Watts, California, as a young black driver was arrested, a bystander was clubbed, and a young woman was seized after being falsely accused of spitting on an officer. A riot broke out, with looting and firebombing of stores. The National Guard was called in, 34 people were killed, hundreds were injured, and 4,000 were arrested. Nonviolence was fading out and being replaced by violence.

In 1967 the U.S. had the most intense riots of its history. The National Advisory Committee on Urban Disorders noted eight major uprisings, thirty-three "serious but not major" outbreaks, and 123 minor disorders. Eighty-three people were killed by gunfire, most of them black. The report profiled the "typical rioter" as a high school drop out who was better educated than the nonrioter, underemployed or employed in a menial job, and angry and hostile toward whites. The report blamed white racism for the disorders. It was an acknowledgement of the problem, but not enough to calm the situation.

Congress responded to the riotous year by passing the Civil Rights Act of 1968, which increased penalties for depriving people of their civil rights. But it exempted police or military people. Opponents of the bill insisted on including tough penalties for anyone who crossed state lines to "organize, promote, encourage, participate in, or carry on a riot," which it defined as any action of three or more people in which there are threats of violence. Ironically the first person to be prosecuted under the law was black: H. Rap Brown, who made a militant speech before a disturbance broke out in Maryland. It was also used against the Chicago Seven (or Chicago Eight) after the anti-war demonstrations during the Democratic Convention.

In 1967, Martin Luther King, Jr. came out against the Vietnam War, expanding his cause from traditional civil rights to broader class and social struggles. At this point he became a target of a concentrated covert attack by the FBI, a campaign designed "to destroy" him in the words of a Senate report of 1976. During this campaign, his phone conversations were tapped, his hotel rooms were bugged, and he was threatened. At one point an FBI letter threatened to release damaging information about him if he did not commit suicide.

When King was killed, it ignited disturbances across the country in which thirty-nine people were killed, thirty-five of whom were black. The FBI intensified its targeting of black leaders, now recognizing them as subversives, even labeling them communists. In late 1969 at 5 a.m., a squad of Chicago police armed with submachine guns and shotguns raided the house of some Black Panthers, firing at least eighty-two rounds, killing two young men, one in his bed. The FBI had an informant among the Panthers who had given them a floor plan of the apartment to help them plan their ambush.

Though it was not known at the time, the government carried out an elaborate covert campaign between 1956 and 1971 called the Counterintelligence Program, or COINTELPRO, It took 295 actions against black groups.

In the early 1970s, the white establishment allowed a few blacks to join the middle class by encouraging "black capitalism" According to Zinn, there was a lot of publicity, but little change. In 1974 the most profitable black corporation was Motown Records, which had sales of forty-five million dollars, while Exxon racked up forty-two billion dollars. Black-owned companies accounted for 0.3 percent of business income.

The Failed Attack on Vietnam

From 1964 to 1972, Zinn points out, the richest country with the largest military force in the world unleashed everything in its arsenal short of nuclear weapons to suppress a nationalist uprising in a poor peasant country and failed. The war incited the most massive antiwar movement in the nation's history.

Vietnam had been under colonial domination of the French since the mid-nineteenth century, but during World War II was occupied by the Japanese Empire. When Japan was defeated in the war, it lost its hold on the country. As the U.S. Defense Department study on Vietnam (the Pentagon Papers) described, the Vietnamese leader Ho Chi Minh united the country with a constitution that borrowed its philosophy and verbiage from the U.S. Declaration of Independence, overthrew the Japanese in 1945 and for a few weeks in September of that year Vietnam was free of foreign domination.

HMMM, THIS ALL MAKES SENSE.

The Allied Powers were eager to remedy that situation and return Vietnam to French control. England occupied the southern part of Indochina and turned it over to the French. Nationalist China under Chiang Kai-shek had occupied the north, and the U.S. persuaded China to turn the North over to the French. In late 1945 and early 1946 Ho Chi Minh wrote eight letters to President Truman. He reminded him of the Atlantic Charter, a document drafted by President Roosevelt and British Prime Minister Winston Churchill that had stated that all countries had a right to self-determination after the war. Truman never responded.

In 1946 the French bombed Haiphong Harbor in an attempt to suppress resistance, but it led to an eight-year struggle, with the U.S. lending massive aid to the French. By 1954 the U.S. had given 300,000 small arms and machine guns and one billion dollars, financing 80 percent of the French campaign. A secret National Security Memo explained why: Communist control of Southeast Asia would imperil U.S. interests in the region, such as rice, tin, rubber, iron ore, coal, and oil.

The U.S. was operating under the Domino Theory; if one country went Communist, others would follow. So it put all its effort into stopping what it saw as the first domino. The Vietnamese wanted self-determination, calling themselves The Democratic Republic of Vietnam. But to the Americans, they were Communists.

When the French gave up the fight in 1954, the U.S. took over. An internationally organized peace negotiation in Geneva decided that the French would withdraw to the south of Vietnam and in two years there would be an election to allow the Vietnamese to choose their own government. The U.S. moved to prevent the unification of the country and set up South Vietnam as a client state of the U.S. under a former Vietnamese official who had been living in New Jersey, Ngo Dinh Diem. He was supported by the U.S. and did its bidding, which included preventing elections. The Pentagon Papers recorded the creation of South Vietnam by the U.S.

Diem was very unpopular, and resistance grew and grew, requiring increasing effort to suppress. When Kennedy took office in 1961, he continued the policies of Truman and Eisenhower, including the authorization of agents to go into North Vietnam to conduct "sabotage and light harassment." Under the Geneva Accords, the U.S. was permitted to have 685 military advisors. Eisenhower secretly sent several thousand, and under Kennedy the number rose to 16,000, some of whom engaged in combat. But the strategy was failing. Most of the territory was in the control of the National Liberation Front, the agency of resistance among the Vietnamese people.

Some South Vietnamese generals plotted to overthrow Diem, discussing their plans with a CIA agent who told U.S. Ambassador Henry Cabot Lodge, who endorsed the idea. Lodge reported to Kennedy's assistant McGeorge Bundy, who reported to the president. Kennedy was hesitant, but made no move to warn Diem. When the rebellion began, Diem called Lodge, who feigned ignorance. Diem tried to flee the palace, but was captured, taken out in a truck, and murdered. Three weeks later Kennedy was assassinated and Lyndon B. Johnson took power.

The generals who took over could not succeed to suppress the Vietnamese, whose resourcefulness and morale was a mystery to American military planners. In August 1964 Johnson used a phony incident in the Gulf of Tonkin to get Congress to authorize him to launch all-out war and began bombing North Vietnam. In 1965, 200,000 troops were sent; the next year added 200,000 more. In early 1968 there were 500,000 troops in Vietnam. The air force was dropping bombs at a higher rate than ever in history. Large areas of South Vietnam were declared free fire zones, which meant anyone in them, including women and children, would be considered the enemy. U.S. actions became increasingly desperate and brutal, but nothing worked to suppress the resistance.

In 1968 Richard Nixon was elected president, promising that he had a secret plan to end the war. He increased the bombing of the North, but planned the "Vietnamization" of the war, which meant to turn it over to South Vietnamese forces with U.S. arms and air support. Nixon secretly spread the bombing into Laos and Cambodia. Then he launched an invasion of Cambodia. It was a failure and Congress began to pull back its support of the war.

Resistance to the war spread and built in intensity. It took many forms, including the disclosure of the Pentagon Papers, an internal Defense Department history of the war made public by Daniel Ellsberg, with editing from Zinn and Noam Chomsky. Nixon claimed to be unaffected by protest, but in fact went berserk over it. It probably impaired his judgment, as in the case when he set up a burglary of Daniel Ellsberg's office. When Nixon invaded Cambodia, protests raged to a peak and at Kent State University in Ohio, National Guardsmen let loose a volley of gunfire on protesting students and killed four of them. Students at four hundred colleges went on strike in protest, the largest such action ever in America.

The protests were uncontrollable, just as the war was unwinnable, and authorities feared that the country was becoming ungovernable. Eventually Nixon was forced to give up, and the war ended. Vietnam had finally won its independence. By the end of the war seven million tons of bombs had been dropped on Vietnam, Laos, and Cambodia, more than double all the bombs dropped on Asia and Europe in World War II. More than 58,000 Americans had been killed, hundreds of thousands were wounded, some very severely, and millions of Vietnamese were killed.

Other Struggles

Out of the civil rights movement and the antiwar movement, grew other movements for liberation and human rights. One of the most significant was the women's movement, which challenged ancient male-dominated social patterns and helped to bring women closer to a position of equality with men. This was an even more intimate revolution, an overturning of values and thought structures not only in the society, but in the family. The oppression of women had gone on so long, was so deeply buried within the psyche of both men and women, that it was largely ignored and accepted. The awareness of the injustices crept up on the society almost undetected, then suddenly burst forth in a new awareness and defiance. What was barely a thought during the civil rights struggles and the anti-war struggles suddenly came into the center stage of history.

Other movements followed, including a push for the recognition of the human rights of prisoners, as guaranteed in the U.S. Constitution. Those rights, as many others, existed on paper, but are often ignored or suppressed in real life. In the early '70s, prisoners revolted inside prisons against cruel and inhumane treatment.

Zinn points out the class structure of the penal system. In 1969, tax fraud cases, involving an average of $190,000, were seen as "white collar crime" and were handled lightly, with only 20 percent of the convicted criminals actually doing jail time. Those sentences averaged seven months. Jehovah's witnesses who refused to serve in Vietnam received two-year sentences. But in burglary or auto theft—the crimes of poor people—the penalties were much harsher. Auto thefts averaging $992 earned sentences of 18 months. Prison uprisings took place with increasing frequency during the late '60s, reaching a peak at Attica State Prison in New York in September 1971. Issues over treatment of prisoners have not made much progress, as conditions may have worsened since that time.

The Native Americans who had stood on the sidelines, pushed off their land by force, trickery, or massacre, began to reassert themselves and their rights during the mid to late twentieth century. The Native American civilization had been effectively destroyed, culture and community shattered, its livelihood taken. Native Americans who had survived were often stripped of their own cultures and pushed into reservations and forced to adopt the trappings of the white culture without its wealth. The U.S. government signed more than 400 treaties with Indians and broke every one. In the late 1960s Indians began to approach the government about the broken agreements. The old struggles resurfaced.

During the same period, homosexuals also began to assert their rights for fair treatment in a movement that came to be known as gay liberation. In the '60s and '70s there was a widespread rebellion against former ways of thinking and doing things. Nearly all conventional beliefs were being subject to scrutiny and examination: the sexual revolution, the environmental move-

142

ment, the psychedelic movement, and various spiritual movements. Music, dress, sexual mores, everything was challenged and changing.

Distrust of officials fomented during the Vietnam War and peaked with the revelation of some of the crimes of the Nixon administration, fueling skepticism and distrust of politicians and all oppressive thinking. Nixon was forced out of office. The Vietnam War was over. The establishment had been pushed back with Vietnam, but the battle was not over. The right wing reconstituted itself.

In the mid-'70s things quieted down. The government ended the military draft, using a volunteer army to leave the fighting to the poor, by making the military one of few viable career choices open to poor people. Consolidation of media into the hands of a few corporations narrowed the range of opinion that was aired in a public forum. The news, the first writings of history, could be controlled by a handful of major corporations controlled by the same power networks that benefitted by defense contracts and other related economic interests.

After the fall of Nixon, power swung to Jimmy Carter, a conservative southern Democrat, then in 1980 to Ronald Reagan, a right wing Republican. But neither party strayed far from a narrowly defined set of principles based on the capitalist belief that: the pursuit of corporate profit is practically the only necessary function of human institutions; profit justifies any behavior; and anything that does not produce a profit does not deserve to exist. The shared belief system of the Republicans and Democrats supported the accumulation of large fortunes by a few, in the midst of crushing poverty, and an acceptance of war as an ongoing activity of the state. Alternatives to those principles were screened out of the two-party system. The axis of power seems to have narrowed with a progression of leaders who all share most of the same beliefs in terms of corporate globalization: Carter, Reagan, Bush, Clinton, and Bush. The disaffection of voters was reflected in abysmally low voter turnout.

In 2000 the Supreme Court stopped the counting of votes in Florida and awarded the presidency to George W. Bush, even though Al Gore had half a million votes more than Bush nationally, and when the votes were finally tallied later by a consortium of newspapers, it was shown that Gore got more votes in Florida than Bush and should have been elected president. But the Supreme Court justices, led by Antonin Scalia, a Bush Sr. appointee, came up with a very strange legal justification for stopping the vote counting based on the 14th Amendment, which ensured "Equal Protection" of the law for all citizens. The majority opinion said that the votes could not be counted because the voting methods were not uniform, some were punch cards, some electronic scanners. That constituted a violation of the principle of Equal Protection, Scalia asserted, because all voters were not using the same systems. But that principle would also have rendered virtually all elections invalid at least since the institution of voting machines. Perhaps because of that, the judgment stated that the decision could never be used as a precedent in any other case, it was just for this one time.

The Hidden Revolution

In the 1990s Zinn reports of the rise of what a New Republic writer called "a permanent adversarial culture" in the United States. In spite of the consensus between Democrats and Republicans that ensured smooth running of capitalism and massive military power in service of the empire, with wealth staying right where it was, in the hands of a few, there were still many people who were not going along with the system. Since the corporate media prefer to deny the existence of discontent or opposition to the status quo, little trace of it can be found in mainstream media channels.

Other Works

Howard Zinn is the author of about twenty books, and innumerable essays, articles, plays, and introductions to other people's books. Following is a listing and discussion of a selection of them.

The Zinn Reader: Writings on Disobedience and Democracy

If *People's History of the United States* is Zinn's principal work, *The Zinn Reader* stands as the other bookend on the Zinn bookshelf. It's a good second pillar in building an understanding of Zinn and his work. It's a brick of a book, nearly 700 pages, stuffed full of essays, articles, selections from books, and autobiographical pieces by Zinn grouped into sections on race, class, war, law, and "means and ends," which refers to activism. The book emerged from a meeting in 1978 when Zinn was teaching in Paris with Dan Simon, the founder of Seven Stories Press. Simon proposed the idea of a book to give people who knew *People's History* a single volume in which they could sample a broad range of his writing and ideas. The book succeeds as a definitive slice from the life and career of Howard Zinn.

You Can't Be Neutral on a Moving Train: A Personal History of Our Times is Zinn's autobiography, another of the primary works that should be on any Zinn bookshelf, and is a remarkably personal look at his life.

Conscience of the Jazz Age: LaGuardia in Congress, Zinn's first published work was developed from his doctoral dissertation, which he wrote during his first two years teaching at Spelman College. It dealt with Fiorello LaGuardia, who was best known as mayor of New York from 1934-1945. The book focuses on his term as a member of the U.S. House of Representatives. He served in Congress from 1917 to 1933, with breaks to serve in World War I and to serve as president of the New York City Board of Aldermen from 1920 to 1921. Zinn's interest in the labor movement led him to LaGuardia. He had been interested in writing about civil rights issues, but his Columbia Professor Henry Steele Commager had discouraged him, saying he should stay away from civil rights and pick a safer subject in order to avoid any barriers to getting his PhD.

In Congress, LaGuardia was an upstart and a troublemaker, out of step with his times as he struggled for the rights of working people during the Roaring Twenties. Zinn saw him as a transitional figure who carried the banner for progressive reform in the years before and during the Great Depression before Franklin D. Roosevelt introduced the New Deal. He stood up for peace, free speech, and the rights of the poor and minorities. He fought to keep down the rising costs of food and rent, supported the rights of workers to strike, and worked for a redistribution of wealth through taxation. Though he was a member of the Republican Party, he was at times called a radical and a socialist.

When the disserta-
tion was published
as a book, the title was
shortened to *LaGuardia
in Congress.* Zinn's next two
books, *The Southern Mystique* and
The New Abolitionists, grew out of his
experiences in the civil rights movement.
Both were published in 1964.

The Southern Mystique began as an article in the winter 1963-1964 issue of *The American Scholar*. An editor with Alfred A. Knopf publishing house liked it and encouraged Zinn to expand it into a book. In it Zinn argues that the most striking development is not that the process of desegregation had begun, but that the mystique of the South was dissolving.

Zinn tried to strip away the mystique and look hard at Southern culture. The mystery of the Southern white was that he was believed to carry this thing called racial prejudice around in his head. Zinn took an existential approach—action. Rather than getting hung up on where the problem came from, he said, let's look at changing behavior by changing the circumstances. Zinn suggested that if the laws were changed it would change behavior and the way people think about the issue. If blacks and whites experience living together under equal rights before the law, they will get to know each other and the strangeness, the mystique will fall away.

Zinn's thinking on the issue traced back to his experience in the service with a sergeant who complained about having to eat with a black man, but would rather do it than go without food. Southerners do care about racial segregation, he said, but they care about other things more, such as their economic security, their place in the community, or avoiding going to jail.

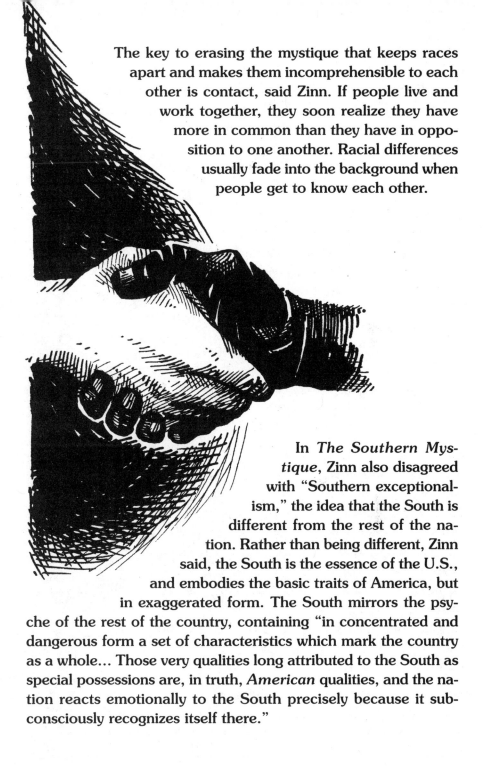

The key to erasing the mystique that keeps races apart and makes them incomprehensible to each other is contact, said Zinn. If people live and work together, they soon realize they have more in common than they have in opposition to one another. Racial differences usually fade into the background when people get to know each other.

In *The Southern Mystique*, Zinn also disagreed with "Southern exceptionalism," the idea that the South is different from the rest of the nation. Rather than being different, Zinn said, the South is the essence of the U.S., and embodies the basic traits of America, but in exaggerated form. The South mirrors the psyche of the rest of the country, containing "in concentrated and dangerous form a set of characteristics which mark the country as a whole... Those very qualities long attributed to the South as special possessions are, in truth, *American* qualities, and the nation reacts emotionally to the South precisely because it subconsciously recognizes itself there."

SNCC: The New Abolitionists. Zinn's third book also grew out of his experience as an adult adviser to the Student Nonviolent Coordinating Committee. The book attempted to "catch a glimpse of SNCC people in action, and to suggest the quality of their contribution to American civilization."

As always, he made no attempt to be an objective outside observer. He was closely involved with SNCC and the book was drawn primarily from his own experiences, as well as his research through SNCC's archives and other available material. He called the organization "the nation's most vivid reminder that there is an unquenchable spirit alive in the world today, beyond race, beyond nationality, beyond class. It is a spirit which seeks to embrace all people everywhere."

He compared SNCC members to the abolitionists, who fought against slavery from the inception of the United States up to the Civil War. "We have in this country today a movement which will take its place alongside that of the abolitionists, the Populists, the Progressives—and may outdo them all," he wrote.

He drew the idea from Erik Erikson, a psychoanalyst who developed a theory on social development and coined the phrase "identity crisis," that a patient in therapy "must begin to see himself as he really is." Applying it to America's civil rights struggles, he said that the "young Negro" in the civil rights movement had forced the country "to see itself through *his* eyes" instead of the Negro always having to view himself through the eyes of the white man" and as a result, America "is coming closer to a realistic appraisal of its national personality."

Zinn also noted differences. The abolitionist movement was led primarily by whites from New England, but the civil rights movement was led by young blacks. The abolitionists mostly relied on persuasion by the written and spoken word; the civil rights activists borrowed methods of nonviolent resistance from Mohandas Ghandi. The new abolitionists demonstrated their messages through "physical acts of sacrifice." When those actions are broadcast around the world by mass media they bring attention and pressure for reform.

The key to understanding abolition old and new, Zinn said, was "the recognition that agitation, however it offends one's friends and creates temporary strife, is indispensable to social progress as a way of breaking through an otherwise frozen status quo."

Black is not a Vice nor is Segregation a Virtue

Zinn said the civil rights movement demonstrated that blacks and whites can live and work together. "Never in the history of the United States has there been a movement where the lives, day by day, of Negro and white people are so entwined physically, intellectually, emotionally." Though relations were not always harmonious, Zinn believed that contact between races was the key to erasing old boundaries.

New Deal Thought. Zinn's fourth book was born in a taxicab after a meeting of the American Historical Association. He shared a cab with another historian, Leonard Levy, who recognized Zinn as the winner of the Beveridge Prize for his book on LaGuardia and offered Zinn the opportunity to edit a volume on the New Deal for a series on American Heritage he and Alfred Young were putting together for Bobbs Merrill Company. Since the book was commissioned rather than his own idea, he considered it of minor importance. It was an editing job, primarily, as opposed to a writing project, though Zinn did write the introductory essay.

His assessment of the New Deal was essentially that it had not gone far enough. It was a step in the right direction, an attempt to deal with some of the inequities that were making life in America increasingly unbearable for ever larger numbers of people. Even the rich were disadvantaged by the crumbling of social systems

MR. PRESIDENT, THINGS WERE GOING SO WELL— WHY'D YOU STOP?

into a general malaise in which the economic system was barely functioning. The ambitious reforms of Roosevelt created a new environment, and made great strides toward fixing what was wrong with the system.

Zinn said the "New Deal's accomplishments were enough to give many Americans the feeling they were going through a revolution." And though the administration "successfully evaded any one of a number of totalitarian abysses into which they might have fallen"—and "left a glow of enthusiasm, even adoration, in the nation at large … when it was over, the fundamental problem remained—and still remains—unsolved: how to bring the blessings of immense natural wealth and staggering productive potential to every person in the land."

By 1939, as war took attention from reform, America fell back into its previous patterns. "The nation was back to its normal state, a permanent army of unemployed; twenty or thirty million poverty-ridden people effectively blocked from public view by a huge, prosperous, and fervently consuming middle class; a tremendously efficient and wasteful productive apparatus." It was efficient because it could produce a great deal of stuff and wasteful because it produced not what was needed but what could make its owners richest.

Zinn concluded that the accomplishments of the New Deal were to "refurbish middle class America, which had taken a dizzying fall in the depression, to restore jobs to half the jobless, and to give just enough to the lowest classes (a layer of public housing, a minimum of social security) to create an aura of good will."

Though he admits it was a harsh judgment on the New Deal, Zinn said any historian is implicitly commenting on the present in his discussion of the past. Zinn assembled a body of excerpts of writing of the main creators the New Deal, including Thurman Arnold, Henry Wallace, David Lilienthal, Harold Ickes, John Maynard Keynes, and Franklin D. Roosevelt.

Vietnam: The Logic of Withdrawal was published in 1967, and was, according to Zinn, the first book to advocate withdrawal from Vietnam. The book developed out of a series of anti-war articles, beginning in 1966 with "Vietnam: Means and Ends," and "Negroes and Vietnam." After working in the civil rights movement and seeing how much the government resisted giving even the most minimal rights to black people in America, Zinn found it very hard to swallow the contention that the U.S. was dropping bombs on Vietnam for the cause of liberty and democracy. He began to break down the feeble logic of the case the government used to justify the war by showing that if the government just gave Vietnam the twenty billion dollars a year it was spending to bomb and strafe it, it would provide five thousand dollars each for every family in Vietnam, families whose yearly income was about seven hundred dollars. The monthly cost of the war was more than the yearly budget of Johnson's anti-poverty program. The war in Vietnam was based on the fallacy that anything was better than Communism, even a dictatorship of wealthy elite over impoverished masses, which is what the U.S. government supported in South Vietnam, as well as in many other third world countries.

One by one Zinn set up the justifications for the war in Vietnam and knocked them down: the idea that it was a battle between Communism and Freedom; the belief that if Vietnam fell to Communism, the rest of the countries of the world would all fall like dominoes stacked in a line; the idea that the U.S. was fighting an outside aggressor in Vietnam. The war was discussed in terms of winning, he said, while the real question was whether we had any moral grounds for being there. What was defined as victory really meant keeping a brutal oligarchy in power.

The book ends with a speech written for President Johnson to give as he pulls out of Vietnam. It was a fantasy never to become real, but Zinn did receive letters from some politicians, including Senator Edward Kennedy, who said only that the book was "very interesting" and Massachusetts' African American Republican Senator Edward Brook, who told Zinn he had "great respect" for the work.

Artists in Times of War, published in 2003, is a small book about how artists can direct their work in the struggle against war and injustice. Artists are not only creators of new things that transcend the conventional boundaries of society, Zinn says; they are also human beings who live in the world, and therefore their art can be used to help to elevate society, to make a difference, and to help alleviate suffering.

Marx in Soho: A Play on History, written in 1999, is a play by Howard Zinn, a one-man show that introduces its audience to Marx, his wife Jenny, his children, and the anarchist Mikhail Bakunin. It's an engaging introduction to Marx's ideas and analysis of social evolution and how vibrant his ideas remain in the twenty-first century.

YOU KNOW, I REALLY AM A NICE GUY ONCE YOU GET TO KNOW ME.

Bibliography: Zinn's Writings

Artists in Times of War (2003) ISBN 1-58322-602-8

The Cold War & the University: Toward an Intellectual History of the Postwar Years (Noam Chomsky (Editor) Authors: Ira Katznelson[8], R. C. Lewontin, David Montgomery, Laura Nader, Richard Ohmann[9], Ray Siever, Immanuel Wallerstein, Howard Zinn (1997) ISBN 1-56584-005-4

Declarations of Independence: Cross-Examining American Ideology (1991) ISBN 0-06-092108-0 [10]

Disobedience and Democracy: Nine Fallacies on Law and Order (1968, re-issued 2002) ISBN 0-89608-675-5

Emma: A Play in Two Acts About Emma Goldman, American Anarchist (2002) ISBN 0-89608-664-X

Failure to Quit: Reflections of an Optimistic Historian (1993) ISBN 0-89608-676-3

The Future of History: Interviews With David Barsamian (1999) ISBN 1-56751-157-0

Hiroshima: Breaking the Silence (pamphlet, 1995) ISBN 1-884519-14-8

Howard Zinn on Democratic Education Donaldo Macedo, Editor (2004) ISBN 1-59451-054-7

Howard Zinn on History (2000) ISBN 1-58322-048-8

Howard Zinn on War (2000) ISBN 1-58322-049-6

Justice? Eyewitness Accounts (1977) ISBN 0-8070-4479-2

Justice in Everyday Life: The Way It Really Works (Editor) (1974) ISBN 0-89608-677-1

LaGuardia in Congress (1959) ISBN 0-8371-6434-6, ISBN 0-393-00488-0

La Otra Historia De Los Estados Unidos (2000) ISBN 1-58322-054-2

Marx in Soho: A Play on History (1999) ISBN 0-89608-593-7

New Deal Thought (Editor) (1965) ISBN 0-87220-685-8

Original Zinn: Conversations on History and Politics (2006) Howard Zinn and David Barsamian ISBN 0-06084-425-6

Passionate Declarations: Essays on War and Justice (2003) ISBN 0-06-055767-2

The Pentagon Papers Senator Gravel Edition. Vol. Five. Critical Essays. Boston. Beacon Press, 1972. 341p. plus 72p. of Index to Vol. I-IV of the Papers, Noam Chomsky, Howard Zinn, editors

A People's History of American Empire (2008) by Howard Zinn, Mike Konopacki and Paul Buhle ISBN 0-80508-744-3

A People's History of the Civil War: Struggles for the Meaning of Freedom by David Williams, Howard Zinn (Series Editor) (2005) ISBN 1-59558-018-2

A People's History of the United States: 1492 – Present (1980), revised (1995)(1998)(1999)(2003) ISBN 0-06-052837-0

A People's History of the United States: Teaching Edition Abridged (2003 updated) ISBN 1-56584-826-8

A People's History of the United States: The Civil War to the Present Kathy Emery Ellen Reeves Howard Zinn (2003 teaching edition) ISBN 1-56584-725-3

A People's History of the United States: The Wall Charts by Howard Zinn and George Kirschner (1995) ISBN 1-56584-171-9

The People Speak: American Voices, Some Famous, Some Little Known (2004) ISBN 0-06-057826-2

Playbook by Maxine Klein, Lydia Sargent and Howard Zinn (1986) ISBN 0-89608-309-8

The Politics of History (1970) (2nd edition 1990) ISBN 0-252-06122-5

Postwar America: 1945 – 1971 (1973) ISBN 0-89608-678-X

A Power Governments Cannot Suppress (2006) ISBN 978-0872864757

The Power of Nonviolence: Writings by Advocates of Peace Editor (2002) ISBN 0-8070-1407-9

SNCC: The New Abolitionists (1964) ISBN 0-89608-679-8

The Southern Mystique (1962) ISBN 0-89608-680-1

Terrorism and War (2002) ISBN 1-58322-493-9 (interviews, Anthony Arnove (Ed.))

Three Strikes: Miners, Musicians, Salesgirls, and the Fighting Spirit of Labor's Last Century (Dana Frank, Robin Kelley, and Howard Zinn) (2002) ISBN 0-8070-5013-X

The Twentieth Century: A People's History (2003) ISBN 0-06-053034-0

Vietnam: The Logic of Withdrawal (1967) ISBN 0-89608-681-X

Voices of a People's History of the United States (with Anthony Arnove, 2004) ISBN 1-58322-647-8

You Can't Be Neutral on a Moving Train: A Personal History of Our Times (1994) ISBN 0-8070-7127-7

A Young People's History of the United States, adapted from the original text by Rebecca Stefoff; illustrated and updated through 2006, with new introduction and afterward by Howard Zinn; two volumes, Seven Stories Press, New York, 2007.

   Vol. 1: Columbus to the Spanish-American War. ISBN 978-1-58322-759-6

   Vol. 2: Class Struggle to the War on Terror. ISBN 978-1-58322-760-2

The Zinn Reader: Writings on Disobedience and Democracy (1997) ISBN 1-888363-54-1

ABOUT THE AUTHOR AND ILLUSTRATOR

David Cogswell is a writer based in Hoboken, N.J. He has written thousands of articles on business, travel, politics, and the arts for various print and online publications, including *Online Journal*, *Democratic Underground*, *Bushwatch*, Indymedia.org, Fortune.com, *Travel Weekly*, the *Hudson Current* and the *Jersey Journal*. He's the author of *Existentialism For Beginners* and *Chomsky For Beginners*, and has contributed pieces to a number of political books, including *Fortunate Son: The Making of an American President*, by J.H. Hatfield; *Ambushed: The Hidden History of the Bush Family* by Toby Rogers; and *America's Autopsy Report*, by John Kaminski.

Joe Lee is an illustrator, cartoonist, writer and clown. A graduate of Ringling Brothers, Barnum and Bailey's Clown College, he worked for many years as a circus clown. He is also the illustrator for many other For Beginners books including: *Dada and Surrealism For Beginners*, *Postmodernism For Beginners*, *Deconstruction For Beginners*, and *Existentialism For Beginners*. Joe lives with his wife, Mary Bess, three cats, and two dogs (Toby and Jack).

THE FOR BEGINNERS® SERIES

AFRICAN HISTORY FOR BEGINNERS:	ISBN 978-1-934389-18-8
ANARCHISM FOR BEGINNERS:	ISBN 978-1-934389-32-4
ARABS & ISRAEL FOR BEGINNERS:	ISBN 978-1-934389-16-4
ASTRONOMY FOR BEGINNERS:	ISBN 978-1-934389-25-6
AYN RAND FOR BEGINNERS:	ISBN 978-1-934389-37-9
BARACK OBAMA FOR BEGINNERS, AN ESSENTIAL GUIDE:	ISBN 978-1-934389-44-7
BLACK HISTORY FOR BEGINNERS:	ISBN 978-1-934389-19-5
THE BLACK HOLOCAUST FOR BEGINNERS:	ISBN 978-1-934389-03-4
BLACK WOMEN FOR BEGINNERS:	ISBN 978-1-934389-20-1
CHOMSKY FOR BEGINNERS:	ISBN 978-1-934389-17-1
DADA & SURREALISM FOR BEGINNERS:	ISBN 978-1-934389-00-3
DECONSTRUCTION FOR BEGINNERS:	ISBN 978-1-934389-26-3
DEMOCRACY FOR BEGINNERS:	ISBN 978-1-934389-36-2
DERRIDA FOR BEGINNERS:	ISBN 978-1-934389-11-9
EASTERN PHILOSOPHY FOR BEGINNERS:	ISBN 978-1-934389-07-2
EXISTENTIALISM FOR BEGINNERS:	ISBN 978-1-934389-21-8
FOUCAULT FOR BEGINNERS:	ISBN 978-1-934389-12-6
GLOBAL WARMING FOR BEGINNERS:	ISBN 978-1-934389-27-0
HEIDEGGER FOR BEGINNERS:	ISBN 978-1-934389-13-3
ISLAM FOR BEGINNERS:	ISBN 978-1-934389-01-0
KIERKEGAARD FOR BEGINNERS:	ISBN 978-1-934389-14-0
LACAN FOR BEGINNERS:	ISBN 978-1-934389-39-3
LINGUISTICS FOR BEGINNERS:	ISBN 978-1-934389-28-7
MALCOLM X FOR BEGINNERS:	ISBN 978-1-934389-04-1
NIETZSCHE FOR BEGINNERS:	ISBN 978-1-934389-05-8
THE OLYMPICS FOR BEGINNERS:	ISBN 978-1-934389-33-1
PHILOSOPHY FOR BEGINNERS:	ISBN 978-1-934389-02-7
PLATO FOR BEGINNERS:	ISBN 978-1-934389-08-9
POSTMODERNISM FOR BEGINNERS:	ISBN 978-1-934389-09-6
SARTRE FOR BEGINNERS:	ISBN 978-1-934389-15-7
SHAKESPEARE FOR BEGINNERS:	ISBN 978-1-934389-29-4
STRUCTURALISM & POSTSTRUCTURALISM FOR BEGINNERS:	ISBN 978-1-934389-10-2
ZEN FOR BEGINNERS:	ISBN 978-1-934389-06-5

www.forbeginnersbooks.com